Fáilte à Paris

A PRACTICAL GUIDE TO VISITING, LIVING AND WORKING IN PARIS, 1992

Fáilte à Paris, Association 1901
Paris 1992

Published by:
Fáilte à Paris, Association 1901, 5 rue des Irlandais, Paris.
tel 43 31 32 65
and
The Columba Press
93 The Rise, Mount Merrion, Blackrock, Co Dublin, Ireland

ISBN 1 85607 050 6

Editor
Liam Swords

Editorial Team:
Prof C.E.J. Caldicott, UCD
Kay Duggan, BSc.HDip., Paris
Fintan Duffy, BArch., Paris
Mary Flynn, OECD, Paris
Máire Henry, BArch., Paris
David Hughes, BArch., Paris
Kate Kelly, OECD, Paris
Mary Cheyrou Lagrèze, OECD, Paris
Carmel McCormack, Bórd Fáilte, Paris
Gearóid Ó hAllmhuráin, PhD, Paris
Dermot Walls, PhD, Paris
Martin Wickham, Apple Computer, Paris
Sr Elizabeth Whyte, Paris

Acknowledgements:
Yvonne Coyne, Prof Louis Cullen, Sr Kathleen Grimes, Joyce Hayes,
Janet Heeran, Declan Hurley, Raphael McGowan, Finnian Ó Luasa,
Prof Breandán Ó Buachalla, Christine Russell, Mark Whelan and the Irish
Embassy, Paris.

Design:
Bill Bolger

Printed in Ireland by Colour Books Ltd., Dublin

CONTENTS

p.5 TRANSPORT — To and from the airport/ Plan de Paris/Métro/ RER/ Bus/ SNCF/ Taxis

11 ACCOMMODATION — Studios/Flats/Rooms/ Hotels/Hostels/Foyers/ Room with a Family/ Religious Accommoda tion/Useful Terminology

24 FOOD — Restaurants/Student Restaurants/Cafés/ Supermarkets/Specialised shops

29 JOBS — Au Pair and Babysitting/ English Language Teaching/ Bilingual Secretaries/Waiters/ Waitresses/ Fast Food/ Supermarkets/ A.N.P.E/ *Inspection du Travail/* Voluntary Work

40 STUDENTS — French Language Courses/ Libraries/ Archives

51 BUREAUCRACY — Residence/WorkingPermits/ConsularServices Passports/ *Fiche d'Etat Civil/ Certificat de Coutume/* Advance of Funds/ Legal Advice/ Notaries/ Driving License/ Missing Persons/ Income Tax/ Paid Vacation Trip/ Pay Slips/ Continuous Professional Training/ Banking

59 COMMUNICATION — Telephone/ Minitel/ Postal charges/ Post Office Account

65 HEALTH — Social Security/Emergencies/ Accidents/ Illness/Poisoning/Ambulances/Hospitals/ Clinics/ Pharmacies/ Dental Care/ Social Security/ Voluntary Health Insurance

72 RELIGION — English Language Churches/ Addresses/ Times

75 STATUTORY RIGHTS — Contracts/ Resignation or Lay Off/ Holidays/ Unemployment Benefits/ Disability Benefit/Sick Pay

78 TOURISM — Museums/ Monuments/ Bus Tours/ Boat Trips/ Walks/ Parks and Gardens/ Cemeteries/ Entertainment/ Theatres/ Cinemas/ Night Clubs/ Day Trips

88 LEAVING PARIS — Giving Notice/ Flat/ Job/ Telephone/ Banks/ Social Security/ Repatriating Personal Belongings/ Animals/ Bills/ Death in France

91 IRISH PUBS

93 USEFUL ADDRESSES — A-Z of Irish and other Services in Paris

Be Prepared

Have you
  your E111?
  your long-form birth certificate?
  enough money?
  (a week costs a minimum of IR£200)
  500frs in cash?
  copies of CV in French with photographs
  (black and white)?
  job or interviews arranged?
  an international student card?
  a phrase book?
  a contact (telephone number)?

Watch out

1. Carry identity at all times.
2. Keep passport, money, credit cards separate. Pickpockets only want cash.
3. Most telephone kiosks don't take money.
4. Taxis don't take four people.
5. French drivers are fast an unpredictable.
6. French red tape — you *are* European.
7. Don't pay rent without a lease.
8. *Au pairs* — check contract and conditions.
9. Many shops shut on Monday.
10. Don't travel alone on the Métro late at night.

Transport

To and from Charles de Gaulle Airport

By train: *ROISSY-RAIL :* After passing through Customs (*Douanes*) look for the signs (in English and French) for the shuttle bus (*navette*) to the RER station. Enter without paying as it is part of the airport services. Its final stop is the RER station (announced over the bus intercom). Buy a ticket for Paris (31frs). This covers all destinations in Paris within Zone 2 area (within the *périphérique* boundary approximately). Trains leave in both directions every 15 mins (approx) from 5.30am-11.30pm and journey takes about 35 mins. Contact in Paris should have provided his/her nearest Métro station. Change from the RER line to the Métro at Châtelet or Gare du Nord. The price is the same for anywhere in Paris. If changing to a bus, bus fare must be paid.

By bus: Air France provides a bus to Paris. The journey takes about 30 minutes and costs 38frs. There are two stops, Charles de Gaulle

Etoile (Arc de Triomphe), and Porte Maillot. From Porte Maillot you can get the Métro to Châtelet les Halles (direction Chateau de Vincennes) or the RER C to Invalides (direction St. Martin d'Etampes/ Dourdan or Massy Palaiseau).

To and from Orly Airport
By train: *ORLY-RAIL* The RER C goes directly to Invalides (direction Montigny Beauchamp), and Versailles (direction St Germain en Yvelines /Versailles RG). Trains run in both directions every 15 mins from 5.30am-10.30pm and the journey takes approx 35 mins. *ORLYVAL* A new connection has been established between Orly Airport and the station Antony (RER B). Trains run from 5.50am-11.48pm every 4-7 mins. One-way ticket costs 55frs. From Antony RER B serves all stations to Paris as far as Gare du Nord.
Using this line it is possible to change between Orly and Charles-de- Gaulle airports. Ticket linking both airports costs 69frs.
See below for instructions on how to use RER and Métro.

By bus: *ORLYBUS* runs every 15 mins between the airport and Denfert-Rochereau. Journey takes 25 mins (approx). Costs 25frs or 6 Métro tickets. *JETBUS* links Orly and Villejuif (Métro ligne 7) and ticket costs 17frs.

Plan de Paris
An essential pocket-sized guide to Paris and widely available. It provides a full index of streets with maps of each *arrondissement*, as well as Métro and RER networks and depending on the edition, lists of administrative buildings, churches, museums, theaters etc, and one-way streets for drivers.

Métro (Underground)
The Métro operates within Paris and its immediate suburbs. Tickets may be purchased individually or in books of 10 (*carnet*). An individual ticket (*un ticket*) costs 5.60frs whereas a *carnet* costs 34.50frs. It is cheaper in the long run to buy a *carte orange* (monthly ticket) per zone or per number of zones required (price list below) which is valid on RER, Métro, bus and SNCF within the number of zones marked on the ticket.

Zones	1 & 2	3	4	5
2nd class	180frs	234frs	323frs	391frs

Carte orange is generally available at tobacconists (*Tabac*)

Other options are available on a daily, weekly or occasional basis. *Formule* 1 is a ticket valid for one day's unlimited travel and costs-

Zones	1 & 2	1,2 & 3	1,2,3 & 4	1,2,3,4 +Roissy/Orly
2nd class	23frs	30frs	43frs	70frs

CARTE PARIS VISITE permits unlimited travel on Métro, bus, RER, and SNCF for a 3 or 5 day period. Zones 1-3 is for travel in Paris and the immediate suburbs. Zones 1-4 is for travel in Paris and the surrounding region (e.g. Versailles, Saint-Germain-en-Laye and Roissy and Orly airports) and costs-

Zones	1-3	1-4
3-day	80frs	150frs
5-day	130frs	185frs

It also offers discounts (20-35%) for several tourist sites (e.g. Tour Montparnasse, Musée Grevin, boat trips on the Seine etc).

CARTE HEBDOMAIRE (weekly card) is valid for 2 trips a day on Métro, RER or bus for 6 consecutive days. Consult local RATP *guichet* for prices.

NB *Carte orange, formule I, carte Paris visite, carte hebdomodaire*, are nominative, i.e. must bear the name of owner. For *carte orange* two photos are required.

Each ticket, once passed through the machine (remember to recuperate it while passing through the barrier, and hold on to it for the duration of journey) is valid for as many journeys and interconnections (*correspondances*) as required, as long as the passenger does not go through the exit (*sortie*) barriers. The tickets may be used in the buses and the RER within Paris.

First use the Métro map to locate required station (most Paris addresses include the nearest Métro stop) and then the line on which the station lies. Follow the colour right through to the last station, note the number of the line, and finally the name of the terminus. Follow the signs bearing this name to find the platform (*quai*). Here, check again from the signs suspended above the platform. To make a connection, locate the station(s) where the change can be affected and apply the same principle.

Note: First class exists only on RER. Tickets may be inspected (*contrôlé*) and a fine issued to holders of second class ticket in a first class compartment. Fines are a minimum of 70frs on the spot, 200frs if unable to pay immediately.

RER *(Réseau Express Régional)*
This is the suburban rapid rail system. While interconnections (*correspondances*) are possible between the Métro and the RER systems, they never share the same platforms. The tickets can be the *carnet* for anywhere in Paris, all the way through to the 5-zone monthly ticket (*carte orange*) which covers a radius of up to 80km outside Paris.

The RER lines frequently fork, so be sure to check that the required station is lit up on the illuminated panels hung above the platform (*quai* or *voie*). The direction, like the Métro, is determined by the terminus station. Unlike the Métro, the RER frequently does not stop at all the stations on its route. If the required station is not lit up, wait for the next train.

Plan du Quartier. Detailed maps of each locality are always displayed in Métro and RER stations (usually at the entrance near the turnstile exit). These maps include a sheet index with house numbers, public buildings and stations clearly marked.

Bus
The bus provides passenger with a much better geographical knowledge of Paris than Métro or RER. The *carte orange* is equally valid on the bus but do not stamp (*composter*) it, just show it to the driver. If the *carnet* is used, the number of tickets to be stamped

---

depends on the length of the journey or the number of sections between starting and stopping points. (There are route maps in the bus indicating this). Otherwise buy the ticket from the driver. Most bus rides require a maximum of two. (*Orlybus* requires six). All tickets, except *carte orange* and *carte jaune*, must be stamped on the bus. Route maps are also displayed in the bus shelters.

The Métro, RER and most buses stop between midnight and 1pm. (Service re-starts at 6am). There is however a skeleton bus service, *Noctambus*, which runs on the hour all through the night and services the main North/South and East/West areas of Paris. The departure point is Place du Châtelet on the right bank just beside Les Halles.

SNCF

The SNCF trains are of two main types: those that service the suburbs (*banlieues*), the *carte orange* being the operative ticket or tickets bought at the desk and the mainline trains for longer journeys (*Grandes Lignes*), i.e. TGV, Corail, etc.

The fare system for mainline trains depends on the time and date of the journey as the price (*tarification*) is based on whether passenger is travelling in a red, blue or white period; red being the most in demand and therefore the most expensive (+ 20%), blue less so and white normal. Try to travel during the white period. All train timetables clearly show these differences. Normally, buy a reservation with the ticket (obligatory on the TGV). The reservation guarantees a seat and costs about 30frs.

Both ticket and reservation card must be stamped before boarding the train. Failure to do this automatically results in a fine on the train. The *machines à composter* are usually at the entrance to the platform.

For those aged 25 and under, the youth card (*carré jeune*) is available and entitles the holder to half-price for mainline tickets. Each *carré jeune* is valid for four journeys and costs 140frs. Both the ticket and one corner of the *carré jeune* must be stamped before each journey.

Carrissimo is a new youth pass which gives price reduction to the holder and up to three companions between the ages of 12 and 25. The pass can be purchased at most train stations for either four (190frs) or eight (350frs) trips *(trajets)*. It is valid in Ist and 2nd class in all trains except certain kinds of TGV. *Trajets* not used will be reimbursed by the SNCF on production of the card.

NB. Half-price ticket must be bought in the station before leaving and both ticket and *carissimo* must be stamped *(compostés)* before entering the platform.

Taxis

Taxis in Paris are abundant and relatively cheap when shared. Normally, they take a maximum of 3 passengers. It is difficult to get them on Friday and Saturday nights.

Accommodation

Accommodation in Paris is hard to find. The main types are, *chambre de bonne* (maid's room), studio/*studette* (one room flat), flat (two or more rooms), hostels/*foyers*, hotel, room with a family.

Finding a place to stay

There are two main ways to find accommodation. One is to use an agency. There are a few agencies who only charge about 400frs, for which they will provide information on available lodgings, flats or studios which the applicant will then have to follow up. Most agencies charge substantially more (12% of the annual rent split between owner and tenant) and all business is done through the agency.

Consult the following publications:
Le Figaro, Thursday's issue (4.50frs)

De Particulier à Particulier, Thursday (12frs)
J'annonce, Wednesday (9frs)
Free Voice , American Church, monthly (free)
Fusac, address below, twice monthly (free)

Also consult the following bulletin boards:
American Church, 65 quai d'Orsay, 75007 Paris M° Invalides
British Institute, 9 rue de Constantine, 75007 Paris M° Invalides
CIDJ, 101 quai Branly 75015 Paris M° Bir-Hakim
Cité Universitaire, 21 bd Jourdain, 75014 Paris M° Porte d'Orléans
CROUS, 39 Av Georges Bernanos, 75005 Paris M° Port-Royal
Fusac, 3 rue Larochelle, 75014 Paris M° Gaité, Edgar Quinet
Irish Chapel, 5 rue des Irlandais, 75005 Paris M° Place Monge, Cardinal Lemoine
St Joseph's Church, 50 ave Hoche, 75008 Paris M° Charles-de-Gaulle
Shakespeare and Company, 37 rue de la Bûcherie, 75005 Paris M° Saint-Michel

What sort of accommodation

Furnished accommodation is usual (and cheaper), but for unfurnished/semi-furnished reasonably priced furniture can be bought at several places: e.g. Samaritaine (M° Louvre) or Conforama (M° Pont Neuf) and IKEA (RER B to Parc des Expositions, free shuttle bus to centre). Cheap second-hand furniture is not widely available but can be found in the local flea market *(marché aux puces)*, or the huge, permanent market at Porte de Clignancourt (same Métro stop). An annual tax *(taxe d'habitation)* must be paid on unfurnished accommodation and is calculated on the size and location of the appartment occupied in January.

Papers

All papers should be in order when flat-hunting (see Administration). Absolutely necessary are: residence permit *(carte de séjour)*, 3 payslips, bank identification (RIB) and possibly a French referee. 3 months rent is usually required upfront, 2 months deposit *(caution)*, and 1 month in advance. The owner is legally required to provide a contract *(contrat de location* or *bail)* and must give a receipt *(quittance de loyer)* for each month's rent paid. Three months notice is required before moving out and the landlord must reimburse the deposit within two months, less deductions for damage caused. All deductions must be justified and a copy of the repair bill provided. Repainting and other general maintenance work is not deductable.

Studios/Flats/Rooms

The cheapest accommodation is small rooms and studios/*studettes*. These range from 1500–2500frs per month for a room and from 2800frs per month and up for a studio. A small appartment *(deux pièces)* starts at 3300frs per month. Anything over this is literally limitless. A useful rule of thumb is to allow 110frs per square metre. e.g. 25m² would be approximately 2750frs. Unfurnished accommodation has a monthly tax *(droit du bail)* of about 80frs.

NB: Legally, *pièce* does not include the kitchen and bathroom, i.e. 2/3/4 *pièces* means kitchen, bathroom plus 2/3/4 rooms.

Charges *(charges comprises cc/ttc)* cover the heating, lighting, water and maintenance of the building. Check advertisement for this as they can add considerably to the rent (300-600frs per month).

Note: In France all water used, hot and cold, must be paid for. The water company takes regular readings. Water counters are usually located under the sink and/or near the bath.

Note: Those experiencing problems with landlords should contact *l'Association des Comités de Défense des Locataires* (A.C.D.L.), 11 rue Bellefond, 75009 Paris, tel 48 78 54 11

Hotels

Recommended only for short stays as they are unacceptable as a fixed address for those seeking residence permits, jobs etc.

Key: S - Single; D - Double. Prices per night.

	Name	Address	Telephone	S	D
1e	**Montpensier	12 rue de Richelieu	42 96 28 50	180	395
	*Richelieu-Mazarin	51 rue de Richelieu	42 97 46 20	160/290	190/290
	*Rouen (de)	42 r.Croix-des-Petits-Champs	42 61 38 21	150/280	170/300
2e	**Vivienne	40 rue Vivienne	42 33 13 26	220/220	275/360
	*Chenier	1 rue Chenier	42 33 92 32	150/200	250/280
	*Sainte Marie	6 rue de la Ville Neuve	42 33 21 61	130/205	160/240
	*Tiquetonne	6 rue Tiquetonne	42 36 94 58	170	200
3e	**France-Europe	112 bd Sebastopol	42 78 75 33	185	320
	**Moderne Hotel Montgolfier	6 rue Montgolfier	42 77 17 61	170/220	270/320
	**Picard	26 rue de Picardie	48 87 53 82	150/280	210/360
	*Bretagne (de)	87 rue des Archives	48 87 83 14	130/280	160/330
	*Grand Hotel Arts et Métiers	4 rue Borda	48 87 73 89	125/200	150/200
	*Sainte-Elisabeth	10 rue Sainte-Elisabeth	42 72 01 66	95/140	160/215
4e	**Andrea	3 rue Saint-Bon	42 78 43 93	150/250	160/290
	**Sevigne	2 rue Mahler	42 72 76 17	214/240	240/310
	*Herse D'Or	20 rue Saint-Antoine	48 87 84 09	130/200	150/200
5e	**Argonautes(des)	12 rue de la Huchette	43 54 09 82	200	300
	**Carmes (des)	5 rue des Carmes	43 29 78 40	115/125	145/360
	**Esmeralda	4 rue Saint-Julien-le-Pauvre	43 54 19 20	95/250	400/500
	**Grand Hotel Moderne	33 rue des Ecoles	43 54 37 78	150/400	180/450
	**Plaisant	50 rue des Bernardins	43 26 83 64	175/400	220/400
	**Studia	51 bd Saint-Germain	43 26 81 00	166/319	166/319
	*Allies(des)	20 rue Berthollet	43 31 47 52	100/130	140/240

	Name	Address	Telephone	S	D
	*Beause Jour-Gobelins	16 av des Gobelins	43 31 80 10	130/180	260
	*Central (Le)	6 rue Descartes	46 33 57 93	130/220	
	*Esperance (de'l)	15 rue Pascal	47 07 10 99	160/220	220/270
	*Flatters	3 rue Flatters	43 31 74 21	160	200
	*Gay-Lussac	29 rue Gay-Lussac	43 5423 96	130/160	170/300
	*Gerson	14 rue de la Sorbonne	43 54 28 40	150/250	240/280
	*Marignan	13 rue du Sommerard	43 25 31 03	110/120	160/170
	*Nevers Luxembourg	3 rue de l'Abbé-de-l'Epée	43 26 81 83	110	190/280
	*Port-Royal	8 bd Port-Royal	43 31 70 06	116/240	147/240
6e	*Academies (des)	15 r. de la Grande Chaumière	43 26 66 44	100/215	175/230
	*Alsace Lorraine	14 rue des Canettes	43 25 10 14	150/300	200/300
	*Buci (de)	22 rue de Buci	43 26 89 22	160	260/320
	*Delhy's	22 rue de l'Hirondelle	43 26 58 25	80/160	160/210
7e	**Eiffel Rive Gauche	6 rue du Gros Caillou	45 51 24 56	145/360	180/390
	**Muguet	11 rue Chevert	47 05 05 93	190/300	210/320
	**Palais Bourbon	49 rue de Bourgogne	47 05 29 26	150/350	150/350
	**Residence Bosquet	19 rue du Champ de Mars	47 05 25 45	160/290	195/290
	**Résidence Orsay	93 rue de Lille	47 05 05 27	170/190	280/390
	*Grand Hôtel Leveque	29 rue Cler	47 05 49 15	170/270	170/270
	*Paix (de la)	19 rue du Gros Caillou	45 55 50 04	118/262	222/285
8e	**Bellevue	46 rue Pasquier	43 87 50 68	185/310	185/310
	**Peiffer	6 rue de l'Arcade	42 66 03 07	110/340	160/340
	**Regence	33 rue Léningrad	43 87 53 82	155/395	350/395
9e	***Comotel	17 rue du Conservatoire	45 23 11 11	185/455	185/485
	**Avenir	39 bd Rochechouart	48 78 21 37	170/200	210/255
	**Belgique	10 rue de Bruxelles	48 74 93 12	155/285	185/375
	**Blanche	69 rue Blanche	48 74 16 94	124/270	143/298
	**Diamond	73 rue de Dunkerque	42 81 15 00	170/210	225/280

Name	Address	Telephone	S	D
**Dieppe (de)	22 rue d'Amsterdam	45 26 74 05	185/200	230/280
**Hollande (de)	4 rue Cadet	47 70 50 79	160/230	200/360
**Montyon	15 rue Montyon	47 70 92 70	140/280	200/350
**Ninon	29 rue Victor Massé	48 74 70 61	180/360	210/360
**Rex	4 bis cité Rougemont	48 24 60 70	160/260	210/360
**Royal Navarin	7 rue Navarin	48 78 51 73	160/260	260/290
**Victor Massé	32 bis rue Victor Massé	48 74 37 53	180/360	210/360
*Athena	16 rue Papillon	47 70 56 43	100/230	150/250
*Perfect	39 rue Rodier	42 81 18 86	105/230	155/230
*Savoy	29 rue de Navarin	48 78 62 66	130/165	165/295
Lille (de)	2 rue Montholon	47 70 38 76	100	120/220

	Name	Address	Telephone	S	D
10e	***Terminus-Est	5 rue du 8 Mai 1945	42 08 58 50	200	250/400
	**Albouy	4 rue Lucien	42 08 20 09	130/260	260/280
	**Champagne	168 rue du fg Saint-Denis	40 37 71 71	I00/150	200/250
	**Europe	98 bd Magenta	40 37 71 15	190/280	220/340
	**Jarry	4 rue Jarry	47 70 70 38	100/210	140/240
	**Liège et Strasbourg	67 bd de Strasbourg	47 70 10 57	160/259	180/290
	**Londres et du Bresil	18 rue de la Fidélité	47 70 72 55	120/220	270/300
	**Nord (du)	47 rue Albert Thomas	42 01 66 00	160/200	240/300
	*Alsace (d')	85 bd de Strasbourg	40 37 75 41	100	150/210
	*Brabant	18 rue des Petits Hotels	47 70 12 32	100/260	100/260
	*Chabrol	46 rue de Chabrol	47 70 10 77	100/180	150/280
	*Cambrai	129 bis bd Magenta	48 78 32 13	82/152	108/152
	*Familles (des)	216 fg Saint-Denis	46 07 75 56	100/140	150/250
	*France (de)	57 rue des Petites Ecuries	47 70 15 83	90/180	170/235
	*Lafayette	198 rue Lafayette	40 36 76 07	100	120/150
11e	**Notre-Dame	51 rue de Malte	47 00 78 76	160/190	260/310
	**Plessis	25 rue du Grand Prieuré	47 00 13 38	190/290	250/290
	*Baudin	113 av Ledru-Rollin	47 00 18 91	100/120	150/250
	*France(de)	159 av Ledru-Rollin	47 00 54 38	140	170/180
	*Sans-Souci	113 bd de Ménilmontant	43 57 00 58	80/120	120/140

	Name	Address	Telephone	S	D
12e	**Chaligny	5 rue Chaligny	43 43 87 04	140/255	160/320
	**Lux Hotel				
	Picpus	74 bd de Picpus	43 43 08 46	130/295	130/295
	**Modern				
	Hotel	98 bis crs de Vincennes	43 43 11 24	125/297	185/360
	**Sport	258 av Daumesnil	43 43 61 36	170/320	170/320
	**Terminus et				
	Des Sports	96 crs de Vincennes	43 43 97 93	100/310	170/310
	*Aveyron (de l')	5 rue d'Austerlitz	43 07 86 86	150/240	150/240
	*Printania	91 av du Dr Arnold			
		Netter	43 07 65 13		130/21
13e	**Arts (des)	8 rue Coypel	47 07 76 32	140/240	150/290
	**Véronèse	5 rue Véronèse	47 07 20 90	145/220	178/255
	*Arian-Hotel	102 av de Choisy	45 87 34 58	110/120	140/230
	*Beaux-Arts (des)	2 rue Toussaint Feron	47 07 52 93	100/230	150/250
	*Lebrun	33 rue Lebrun	47 07 97 02	100/150	150/220
	*Sthrau	1 Sthrau Angle	45 83 20 35	100/220	130/220
14e	**Daguerre	94 rue Daguerre	43 22 43 54	175/205	205/340
	**Home Fleuri	75 rue Daguerre	43 20 02 37	170/290	170/290
	** Midi (du)	4 av René Coty	43 27 23 25	188/328	188/328
	*Celtik	15 rue d'Odessa	43 20 93 53	130/160	200/220
	*Ouest	2è rue de Gergovie	45 42 64 99	110/150	150/200
	*Telemaque	64 rue Daguerre	43 20 33 29	120/140	150/190
15e	**Modern				
	Vaugirard	14 rue Petel	48 28 53 96	170/180	180/330
	**Royal				
	Lecourbe	286 rue Lecourbe	45 58 06 05	170/270	170/270
	*Mont Blanc	11 bd Victor	48 28 16 79	140/200	165/290
16e	**Villa D'Auteuil	28 rue Poussin	42 88 30 37		150/255
	*Résidence				
	Chalgrin	10 rue Chalgrin	45 00 19 91	120/230	130/390
	*Ribera	66 rue Lafontaine	42 88 29 50	140/220	160/260
17e	**Cabourg	5 rue Mont Dore	45 22 41 23	180/330	220/380
	**Deux Avenues	38 rue Poncelet	42 27 44 35	190/300	190/300

	Name	Address	Telephone	S	D
17e	**Quietude	18 rue Berzélius	46 27 25 19	200/240	280
	**Wagram	3 rue Brey	43 80 15 52	165/365	220/390
	*Niel	11 rue Saussier Leroy	42 27 99 29	160/260	180/280
	*Santana	109 rue Legendre	46 27 60 40	100/130	180/240
18e	**André-Gill	4 rue André Gill	42 62 48 48	150/290	200/290
	**Anvers (d')	74 bd Rochechouart	42 57 07 20	180	220/230
	*Beausejour	1 rue Lepic	46 06 45 08	95/95	140/185
	*Central	110 rue Damrémont	42 64 25 75	90/160	110/160
	*Tholozé Montmartre	24 rue Tholozé	46 06 74 83	100/130	180/250
	*Titiana	70 bis bd Ornano	46 06 43 22	120/135	120/240
	Sofia	21 rue Sofia	42 64 55 37	160/180	200/220
19e	**Laumière (le)	4 rue Petit	42 06 10 77	190/270	210/300
	*Polonia	3 rue de Chaumont	42 49 87 15	135/220	150/220
	Atlas	12 rue de l'Atlas	42 08 50 12	120/150	160/220
20e	**Lyanes Village	16 rue des Lyanes	43 61 43 69	250	280
	*Ermitage	42 bis rue de l'Ermitage	46 36 23 44	95/170	160/240
	Eden	7 rue J.B. Dumay	46 36 64 22	160/160	190/260

Note: All 3-star, 2-star and 1-star hotels have lifts and provide telephone and TV in each room.

Further information: Hôtels Paris 1991-1992, Office du Tourisme et des Congrès, 127 Champs-Elysées, 75005 Paris, tel 47 23 61 72

Hostels/Foyers

In France not all hostels are reserved for students, some also take young workers. Some offer full or half board. Others provide only bed and breakfast. Prices vary between 60-100frs for bed and breakfast and 1700-2300frs a month for half-board.

The following organisations provide information on hostels.

CIDJ, 101 quai Branly, 75015 Paris, tel 45 66 40 20

Logis de France, 34 Godot de Mauroy, 75009 Paris, tel 40 73 03 61

Fédération Nationale des Logis de France, 23 rue Jean Mermoz, 75008 Paris, tel 43 59 91 99

Associations pour le logement des étudiants et des jeunes travailleurs, 12-14 rue l'Eglise, 75015 Paris

Centre International de séjour, 6 ave Maurice Ravel, 75012 Paris

Association Catholique des services de la jeunesse feminine, 63 rue Monsieur le Prince, 75006 Paris, tel 43 26 92 84

Union nationale des maisons d'étudiants (UNME), 15 rue Ferrus, 75014 Paris, tel 45 89 38 35

Union des Foyers de jeunes travaillers, 12 av de Général-de-Gaulle, 94304 Vincennes, tel 43 74 53 56

Accueil des Jeunes en France (AJF)

This group has four accommodation and information offices in Paris for individual young travellers. They guarantee to find every young traveller decent and low cost lodging.

AJF Plateau Beaubourg (opposite Pompidou Centre), 119 rue St Martin, 75004 Paris, tel 42 77 87 80 M° Châtelet les Halles, Hôtel de Ville.

AJF Quartier Latin, 139 bd St Michel, 75005 Paris, tel 43 54 95 86 M° Port Royal.

AJF Gare du Nord, Halles des Arrivés (Arrivals Hall) 75010 Paris, tel 42 85 86 19 M° Gare du Nord.

AJF Hotel de Ville, 16 rue du Pont Louis Philippe, 75004 Paris, tel 42 78 04 82 M° Hôtel de Ville.

Youth hostels

Youth Hostel card useful. Book ahead. Hostels and foyers set their own ground rules; most have "curfew" hours usually between 11pm and midnight. They are pricier than flats for long stays but provide meals except at weekends.

Students

Selected list by *arrondissement:* (F)-Filles (G)-Garçons (M)-mixte 17/25-age DP-half-board S-Single D-Double S/S-Self-service *-Also accepts Young Workers

Address	Telephone	Information	S	D
1er 18 rue Jean-Jacques Rousseau	45 08 02 10	G 17/23 P DP	4500frs	4000frs
3e * 11 bd Filles du Calvaire	42 72 00 89	F 18/24 kitchen		1150frs
4e * 7 rue Poulletier	46 33 33 98	F 18/23 DP	2400frs	2050frs
21 rue Saint Antoine	42 77 95 02	G 16/20 DP		
5e * 41 rue Lhomond	47 07 60 94	F 17/21 DP		
21 rue Daubenton	47 07 07 39	F 17/25 DP		

	Address	Telephone	Information	S	D
	41 rue Tournefort	43 36 58 98	M	1860frs	1560frs
	5 rue Amyot	43 31 55 31	F 16/22	2000frs	
	269 rue Saint-Jacques	43 26 46 26	M 16/30	2500frs	1650frs
	5 rue des Irlandais	45 35 59 79	M	2900frs	
6e	46 rue de Vaugirard	46 33 23 30	M 18/25	2356frs	2170frs
	44 rue du Cherche-Midi	45 48 15 05	F 18/22	1800frs	1450frs
	61 rue Madame	45 48 29 06	M 18/25 DP	2850frs	2250frs
	10 rue de Condé	43 29 91 62	F 17/19 DP	2800frs	2365frs
	*63 rue Monsieur le Prince	43 26 97 66	F 18/22 DP		
	83 rue de Sèvres	42 22 30 99	F 17/22 DP	2500frs	2250frs
	49 rue de Vaugirard	45 48 82 54	F 18/25 DP	2800frs	2500frs
	104 rue de Vaugirard	45 49 26 25	M 18 +		
7e	21 rue du Général Bertrand	47 34 29 72	F 18/25 DP	3150frs	3000frs
	52 rue Vaneau	42 22 46 06	F 17/25 DP		
8e	*22 rue de Naples	45 22 23 49	F 18/24 DP	2170frs	1810frs
	*28 av Georges V	47 23 35 32	F 18/25		
	*29 rue du Dr Lancereaux	45 62 18 72	F 18/23		
9e	14 rue de Calais	48 74 71 90	F 18/21 DP	3400frs	
	*14 rue de Trévise	47 70 90 94	G 18/26 DP	1630frs	1520frs
10e	8 rue Alexandre Parodi	46 07 71 38	F 18/22 DP	1800frs	1350frs
11e	15 rue Villermé	47 00 01 44	F 17/23 DP	2450frs	1650frs
	*20 bd Voltaire	47 00 59 99	F 16/22 DP	2175frs	2000frs
	*94 rue Charonne	43 71 11 27	F 18/35	1680frs	1130frs
	123 bd Charonne	43 79 07 73	M 18/20 DP	1925frs	1530frs
13e	*243 rue de Tolbiac	45 89 06 42	F 18/25 P	2470frs	2240frs
14e	61 bd Saint-Jacques	45 65 29 74	F 22+	2050frs	1650frs
	*24 rue Liancourt	43 22 47 60	F 18/26	1342frs	984frs
	9 rue de Moulin-Vert	45 40 96 59	F 18/25	2150frs	
	214 bd Raspail	40 47 05 47	F 18/22 DP	2659frs	2500frs
	6 rue Jean Dolent	43 36 36 66	G		
	*86 rue de Gergovie	45 42 51 2	F 18/28 DP	2700frs	2070frs
	34 av Reille	45 89 15 51	M 20/27		
15e	101 rue Olivier de Serres	48 28 21 38	F 17/25 DP	1838frs	
	8 rue Carcel	48 28 25 50	F 16/22 DP	2400frs	2000frs
	3 rue Antoine Bourdelle	42 22 99 23	F 17/24 DP	2850frs	
	168 rue Blomet	45 33 48 21	F 18/24 DP	2235frs	1780frs
	27 rue Dantzig	45 31 12 16	G 18/25 DP	1900frs	
	7 rue Eugène Meillon	45 31 88 55	M all ages		
16e	58 rue Saint Didier	47 27 96 95	F 17/25 DP	2700frs	2135frs
	26 bis rue de Lubeck	47 27 49 15	F 17/22 DP	3080frs	2200frs
17e	24 rue Guillaume Tell	46 22 92 89	M 18/24	1800/2100frs	
18e	*9 rue Georgette Agutte	46 27 05 72	F 18/26 DP	2855frs	2475frs
	*37 rue Eugène Carrère	42 64 97 22	F 18/30 S/S	1200frs	1000frs
19e	*97 rue de Meaux	42 08 86 88	F 18/30 S/S	1540/1610frs	

Address	Telephone	Information	S	D
*59 av Mathurin Moreau	42 38 54 52	F 18/25 DP		2000frs
20e *65 rue Orfila	46 36 82 80	F 18/24 DP	2200frs	1750frs
11 square Monsoreau	43 70 21 04	M 18/25		

Further information:
Foyers pour étudiantes et étudiants (CROUS de Paris, 39 av Georges Bernanos, 75005 Paris, tel 40 51 36 00 M° Port-Royal
Logement de l'étudiant juin 1991 (Centre d'Information et de Documentation Jeunesse CIDJ, 101 quai Branly, 75015 Paris, tel 45 66 40 20 RER Champ de Mars
Lists are also available from:
Association Catholique des Services de la Jeunesse Femme, 63 Monsieur le Prince, 75006 Paris, tel 43 26 97 66, RER Luxembourg
Union Nationale des Maisons d'Etudiants(UNME), 15 rue Ferrus, 75014 Paris, tel 45 89 38 35, M° Glacière

Young Workers

	Address	Telephone	Information & Métro
5e	12 rue des Ecoles	43 29 98 41	F 18/24; M° Maubert-Mutualité
	36 rue des Ecoles	43 29 09 10	F 18/25; M° Cardinal Lemoine
6e	91 rue de Sèvres	45 48 00 30	F 18/24; M° Vaneau/Duroc
	7 bis rue Duguay Trouin	45 48 51 91	F 17/22; M° Saint-Placide
7e	159 rue de l'Université	45 55 80 64	F 17/24; M° Alma-Marceau
8e	9-11 av Beaucour	45 62 55 10	M 18/23; M° Ternes/Etoile
9e	25C rue de Maubeuge	42 85 24 20	G 18/25; M° Cadet
	11 rue Dupérré	45 83 68 27	M (appartments); M° Pigalle
10e	11 rue Gabriel Laumain	47 70 58 46	M 18+ (98 studios); M° Bonne-Nouvelle
11e	165 rue de Charonne	43 71 94 08	M 18/25; M° Charonne
	51 bd de Belleville	43 57 25 61	M 18+; M° Couronnes
	15 rue Crespin du Gast	43 57 44 30	F 25+; M° Ménimontant
12e	61 rue de la Gare de Reuilly	43 45 65 95	F 17/24; M° Daumesnil
	105 bd Diderot	43 72 64 28	F 18/23; M° Nation
13e	24 rue Péan	45 83 17 60	M 18/25; M° Porte d'Ivry
	45 bd Auguste Blanqui	45 35 33 07	M 17/25; M° Place d'Italie
	53 rue des Ternes au Curé	45 86 02 32	M; M° Porte d'Ivry

Address	Telephone	Information & Métro
95 rue du Chevaleret	45 83 68 27	M 18+; M° Chevaleret
52 rue Bobillot	45 89 46 00	G 18/23; M° Tolbiac
22 rue des Malmaisons	45 84 14 61	M 18/24; M° Porte d'Italie
31 rue Daviel	45 89 44 07	M 16/25; M° Glacière
14e 41 rue Didot	45 43 21 56	M 18/25; M° Pernety/Alésia
64 rue de la Santé	45 65 21 50	F 18/25; M° Glacière
48 rue Amiral Mouchez	45 83 68 27	M (studios); M° Cité Universitaire
15e 42 rue des Volontaires	47 83 20 23	F 18/23; M° Volontaires
29 rue de Lourmel	45 77 46 50	G 16/18; M° Dupleix
3 square Léon Guillot	48 28 88 82	F 18/23; M° Convention
7 rue Meilhac	47 83 28 30	F 18+; M° Commerce
5 av Sainte Eugénie	42 50 45 74	F 18/23; M° Convention
46 rue Violet	45 79 45 04	F 18/24; M° Emile Zola
16e 10 rue Alfred de Musset	46 47 78 38	M 18/22; M° Exelmans
154 av Victor Hugo	47 27 24 88	F 17/23; M° Trocadéro
19e 70 rue de la Villette	42 41 81 08	M (studios); M° Belleville
20e 54 rue de Ménilmontant	43 66 85 17	M 18/25; M° Ménilmontant
43 rue du Borrégo	43 64 68 13	M 16/35; M° Télégraphe
12 rue d'Annam	47 97 36 42	M 18+; M° Gambetta
186 bd de Charonne	43 73 28 97	M 18+; M° Ledru Rollin

Note:
Complaints about hotels should be made directly to **Directeur des Industries Touristiques**, 17 rue de l'Ingenieur Keller, 75015 Paris, tel 45 75 62 16

Further information:
Logement des Jeunes Travailleurs (Centre d'Information et de Documentation Jeunesse), 101 quai Branly, 75015 Paris, tel 45 66 40 20, RER Champ de Mars

A room with a family

This is often arranged between friends/family or on recommendation. Some places are advertised in papers (see list above). However, except when housework (normally 12 hours per week) is being done in exchange for the room, prices seem to vary between 1500 and 2000frs per month. English language instruction and conversation sessions are also acceptable currency.

Priests, religious, seminarians

Some religious houses offer accommodation to religious and clergy at very moderate rates.

Les Rédemptoristes, 170 bd Montparnasse, 75015 Paris, tel 43 20 36 20.
Missions Etrangères, 128 rue du Bac, 75007 Paris, tel 45 48 19 92.
Congrégation du St Esprit, 30 rue Lhomond, 75005 Paris, tel 47 07 49 09.
Foyer Sacerdotal, 1 rue Jean Dolent, 75014 Paris, tel 47 07 41 09.

Useful terminology

ascenseur - lift
cuisine - kitchen
entrée - hall
pièce - room
porte blindée - burglar proof door
balcon - tiny balcony
cheminée - fireplace
locataire - tenant
loyer - rent
rez de cour - sub basement level
volets - window shutters

cave - cellar
cuisine américaine - fitted kitchen
kitchenette - kitchen in a cupboard
salle de bains - bathroom
grenier - attic
terrasse - proper balcony
pierre de taille - old stonework
propriétaire - owner
sous sol - basement
rez de chausée - ground floor
mansardé - under the eaves

immeuble standing/grand standing - upmarket building
prix justifié - it's in the 16th or better, you have to pay for it.

Tenants who have problems with their landlords can contact the **Association des Comités de Défense des Locataires (ACDL) 11 rue Bellefont, 75009 Paris tel 48 78 54 11 M° Poissonière.**

Further Information:
Let's Go, Paris pas cher, Pauper's Paris.

Food

Restaurants

In Paris, there is a great choice of restaurants to suit all pockets and tastes. Most restaurants are open for lunch from 12am to 2.30pm and in the evening from 7 to 10.30pm. *Brasseries* complement restaurants by offering a similar but continuous service and some restaurants such as the chain *Hippopotamus* are open until later than normal. Usually the menu and prices are posted outside the restaurant.

Most offer a *formule* or fixed menu which can often be good value. Sometimes this *formule* is only served at midday. Check availability and price before ordering. A *formule* includes a starter, main course and dessert. Extras such as apéritif, wine, mineral water and coffee can add up to give a startling increase in price. Ordering a jug *(pichet)* of house wine *(vin de maison)* is often considerably cheaper than ordering a bottle of wine and likewise asking for a jug of water *(carafe d'eau)* instead of mineral water (e.g. Vittel, Badoit).

The following is a selection by *arrondissement* which offers under 80frs menus.

1er **l'Incroyable,**
26 rue de Richelieu
M° Palais Royal

2e **Christiane**
5 rue de Louvois
M° Quatre Septembre

2e **La Patata**
23 bd des Italiens
M° Opéra

4e **Dame Tartine**
2 rue Brise Miche
M° Hôtel de Ville

5e **Le Baptiste**
11 rue des Boulangers
M° Jussieu

6e **Le Petit Saint Benoît**
4 rue St Benoît
M° St Germain des Prés

6e **Le Petit Vatel,**
5 rue Lobineau
M° Odéon

7e **Chez Germaine**
30 rue Pierre Leroux
M° Vaneau

8e **Chez Mélanie**
27 rue du Colisée
M° Franklin Roosevelt

9e **Chartier**
7 rue du Fbg
Montmartre
M° Rue Montmartre

9e **Hatelet,**
23 rue de Maubeuge
M° Cadet

9e **Hatelet,**
16 rue N.D.de Lorette
M° N.D.de Lorette

9e **Lou Cantou,**
35 cité d'Antin
M° Chaussée d'Antin

10e **Buffet Bonne Nouvelle,**
57 rue d'Hauteville
M° Bonne Nouvelle

10e **Hatelet,**
89 rue d'Hauteville
M° Poissonnière

11e **Hatelet,**
54 rue de Malte
M° République

11e **Val de Loire (Le),**
149 rue Amelot
M° Oberkamph

11e **Le Petit Keller,**
13 rue Keller
M° Ledru Rollin

14e **Le Biniou,**
3 av du Général Leclerc
M° Denfert Rochereau

14e **Mélodine,**
80 av du Général Leclerc
M° Alésia

14e **Au Rendez-Vous des Camionneurs,**
34 rue des Plantes
M° Alésia

15e **Le Blavet,**
75 bis rue de Lourmel
M° Charles Michels

15e **Sampieru Corsu,**
12 rue de l'Amiral Roussin
M° Cambronne

15e **Ty Breiz,**
52 bd de Vaugirard
M° Montparnasse

16e **Self Longchamp,**
111-113 rue Lauriston
M° Boissière

17e **Cafetéria Monte Carlo,**
9 av de Wagram
M°-RER Charles de Gaulle

Note: Lunch menus (40-50frs) are much cheaper than dinner menus.

Employers often issue meal tickets (*ticket restaurant/repas,chèque déjeuner*) . They usually have a face value of 30frs, where both employer and employee have paid half (deductions are made from salary at the end of the month). These tickets are accepted in restaurants,*cafés, traiteurs,boulangeries,* where the ticket symbol is displayed in the window. In most cases the ticket has to be used for its full value. In some cases you can ask for a credit note *(un avoir)* for the balance.

Student Restaurants

Most student restaurants are found in the student quarters of Paris, mainly the 5th and 6th *arrondissements*. They offer a basic meal but good value, 11.50frs for a student and 18.40frs for those with *cartes jeunes*. Several meal tickets can be bought at anytime to avoid large queues for tickets.

> **Assas,** 92 rue d'Assas, 75006 M° Notre-Dame-des-Champs
> **Chu Bichat,** 16 rue Henri Huchard, 75018 M° Porte Saint Ouen
> **Bullier,** 39 av Georges Bernanos, 75005 M° Port-Royal
> **Censier,** 31 rue Geoffroy Sainte Hilaire, 75005 M° Censier-Daubenton
> **Châtelet,** 10 rue Jean Calvin 75005 M° Censier-Daubenton
> **Citeaux,** 45 bd Diderot, 75012 M° Gare de Lyon
> **Clignancourt,** rue Francis de Croisset, 75018 M° Pte de Clignancourt
> **Cuvier-Jussieu,** 8 bis rue Cuvier, 75005 M° Jussieu
> **Dareau,** 13-17 rue Dareau, 75014 M° Saint-Jacques
> **Dauphine,** av de Pologne, 75016 M° Porte Dauphine
> **Grand Palais,** Cours la Reine, 75008 M° Champs Elysées
> **I.U.T.,** 143 av de Versailles, 75016 M° Chardon Lagache
> **Mabillon,** 3 rue Mabillon, 75006 M° Mabillon
> **Mazet,** 5 rue Mazet, 75006 M° Odéon
> **Chu Necker,** 156 rue de Vaugirard, 75015 M° Pasteur
> **Chu Pitié,** 105 bd de l'Hôpital, 75013 M° Saint-Marcel
> **Tolbiac,** 17 rue Tolbiac, 75013 M° Chevaleret

There is a large selection of fast food restaurants such as McDonalds and Quick. There is a sit-down price *(prix sur place)*, and a takeaway price *(prix à emporter)*.

Cafés

Cafés normally serve sandwiches, salads, non-alcoholic and alcoholic beverages and meals throughout the day. Prices vary considerably depending on location and most cafés have higher prices after 10pm. In most cafés there are two prices, one for sitting down *(prix en salle)* and one for standing at the counter/bar *(prix au comptoir)*. The latter is less expensive. Check the price list usually posted outside or at the bar *(tarif des consomations)*.

Beware of cafés in tourist areas. Be very precise when ordering. For example, a glass of beer is commonly known as a *demi-bière* (25 cl), but often you will be served a *demi-litre* (50 cl). Draught beer *(pression)* is also cheaper than bottled beer and it is usually necessary to state your preference, e.g, *un demi-Heineken pression*. The house draught is always cheapest and is often simply known as *un demi pression*. A small black coffee is called *un express* or simply *un café*. *Un express* with a drop of milk is called a *noisette*, a milky coffee is either *café au lait* or *café crème*. Differentiate between a small and a big cup of milky coffee by asking for *petit* or *grand*, the difference in price often being more than double. When sitting down the receipt is issued with the order and the waiter is paid before leaving (or before he goes for his tea-break). At the counter ask for the bill before leaving. Service charges (15%) are included in prices, so tipping *(pourboire)* is not usual.

Supermarkets etc

For food in general, there are three kinds of outlets: supermarkets, street markets, small stores. *Prisunic, Monoprix, Franprix ,Codec* are some examples of good quality supermarkets at good value. There are two kinds of street market: those which are essentially shopping streets *(rues commerçantes)* with many small stores (open daily) e.g. rue Mouffetard; and those which are markets held two or three days a week in various places, e.g. Place Maubert Mutualité, Tuesday, Thursday and Saturday (mornings only). Small grocery stores can be found anywhere and usually carry the name of the chain, e.g. *Codec, Félix Potin*. They often stay open later than normal and are always more expensive. Most expensive are those that open seven days a week and until late at night.

Except for large supermarkets and, most stores are closed on Sundays and Mondays. Note that many businesses close completely for the month of August and leave Paris for the tourists. Local stores usually close for lunch, 1-4pm but remain open until 7.30pm.

There are many specialised shops selling only one line of product:

Boulangerie - bakery   *Pâtisserie*- cake shop
Boucherie- butcher   *Charcuterie- Traiteur* -Delicatessen
Laiterie-Crémerie-Fromagerie- Dairy products *Poissonerie*- Fishmonger
Vins cave- Wine shop (wines, spirits, beers)
Produits de régime/Produits naturels/Produits diététiques- natural and macrobiotic foods
Tabac- Cigarettes,tobacco,postal stamps *(timbres)*, fiscal stamps *(timbres fiscals)*, carnet, *télécartes*.

Most of above close for a month in Summer, July or August. Usually one or two stay open to keep the custom of the area. They will all have notices indicating the nearest alternative shop to them.
For greasy fry and sliced pan, try Marks and Spencer, 35-41 Bd Haussmann, 75008 Paris M° Havre-Caumartin.

Don't forget that metric units apply throughout. Almost everything is sold by the kilo. In markets and cafés always check the change before leaving.

Further information:
Let's Go, Paris Pas Cher, Paupers' Paris

JOBS

Au Pair/ Babysitting

Au Pair. This system permits a student to work in a French family for 30 hours a week plus 2 nights a week 'babysitting' in exchange for accommodation, food, pocket money (1,800frs per month) and *'carte orange'* (190frs) The *au pair* is required to attend French language classes in order to make it possible for the employer to declare her/him for health insurance.

It is also possible for a student to have an accommodation exchange arrangement, i.e. 12 hours work per week in exchange for accommodation only. This can be a very satisfactory arrangement for a student who has work elsewhere without accommodation. Extra hours are generally paid at 35frs per hour.

Babysitting . Many French families need babysitters on Wednesday afternoons when the children are home from school, or at night if the parents go out. The current rate is 35frs per hour. Before undertaking to babysit at night make arrangements with the family regarding the time of return and transport home. The babysitter should be (a) driven home, or (b) provided with a paid taxi, or (c) accomodated over night. Late night travel on public transport can be dangerous and should be avoided. (For late night transport, see page 3).

If interested in babysitting, contact **Foyer Notre Dame**, 26 bis rue de Lubeck, 75016 Paris, tel 47 27 49 15 M° Iéna or Boissière. **C.I.D.J.** also provide a list of au pair agencies. (see page 39.)

English Language Teaching

There are over one hundred private language schools in Paris. They teach English to adults, often business and technical English as well as conversational English. A list of these schools can be obtained at the **British Council**, 9 rue de Constantine, 75007 Paris, tel 45 55 95 95, M° Invalides or from the **C.I.D.J.**, 101 Quai Branly, 75015 Paris,75015 Paris,tel 45 66 40 20. M° Bir Hakeim.

The British Council has an English teaching resource centre where one can borrow books, cassettes, videos, etc. It also has a reference library. The Council organises seminars for teachers.

It is a good idea to do a TEFL (Teaching English as a Foreign Language) course and obtain a certificate. Such courses are offered by the VEC's adult education section and other language schools in Ireland. Experience (one year minimum) is most important. In Paris it is possible to study for a TEFL certificate at the British Council and at WICE, 20 bd du Montparnasse, 75015 Paris, tel 45 66 75 50, M° Duroc. Some schools train teachers to use their own particular method, such as Berlitz, 29 rue de la Michodière, 75002 Paris,tel 47 42 46 54 M° Opéra (contact Julie Huxter). This school has a 12-day training course for which there is no charge but also no remuneration, as do other schools. Berlitz recruit all year round, but generally the best time to look for work is in September/October. Berlitz offer a guaranteed minimum salary for ninety 45-minute units per month, even if only one unit is worked. Each unit is paid at about 50frs (19% Social Security and insurance is deducted from this).

Some schools pay from 50-150frs per hour, depending on experience, location of the school, etc. In some schools, holiday pay is included in this. Sometimes the school will send the teacher to work in companies and pay him/her only for the actual teaching hours, not the time spent travelling which is often considerable.

The best kind of contract to have is a full-time one with a set monthly salary. This is usually about 30 hours work per week, about 24 of which are spent teaching and the rest on preparation and administration.

Expect about 7000frs gross upwards, depending on age, qualifications and experience, e.g. basic 20hrs per week contract, (1) 7700frs-7900frs per month for TEFL cert, (2) 8300frs per month for TEFL diploma + 2yrs experience; over 20hrs rate, 94frs per hour (cert), 100frs per hour (diploma). It is possible to bargain. Fluency in French is not necessary except in some French-run schools. Most schools use the same books with which one should become familiar.

A prepared CV should be sent to the schools before coming to Paris, giving a Paris telephone number. Once arrived, call the different schools.

English can also be taught privately. The going rate is 60-100frs per hour. Place an ad in the local paper, or on the window of a local shop, on the bulletin boards in the Irish Chapel, American Church, British Council (downstairs), St. Joseph's, etc. Another way of teaching privately is by giving telephone lessons.

English Language Schools

	Name	Address	Telephone
1e	Institut d'Enseignement	31 rue Etienne	42 33 35 84
	Pigier	5 rue Saint Denis	42 33 44 88
	Executive Languages		
	Services	25 bd Sébastopol	42 36 32 32
3e	SPLEF	2 rue Gabriel Vicaire	48 87 62 26
	Wall Street Institute	43 rue Beaubourg	48 04 82 02
4e	AVL	28 bd Sébastopol	42 77 39 29
	CLE Langues	15 rue de la Cerisaie	42 76 09 40
	Institut Silc		
	de la Bretonnerie	5 rue Ste Croix de la Bret.	48 87 60 11
	Regency Langues	1 rue Ferdinand Duval	48 04 99 97
5e	Objectifs Langues	36 rue des Boulangers	46 34 11 14
	AC3 Formation Conseils	26 bis rue du Cardinal Lemoine	43 54 30 43
6e	ILC	20 passage Dauphine	43 25 40 55
	English Unlimited	123 bd Montparnasse	43 20 84 64
7e	Inlingua	109 rue de l'Université	45 51 46 60
	British Institute	9/11 rue de Constantine	45 55 71 99
8e	ACF-Speakwell	26 rue Washington	45 63 31 77
	Cours George V	7 rue Marbeuf	47 20 8125
	Ecole Nickerson	26 rue de la Tremoille	47 23 36 03
	Forma Langues	106 bd Haussmann	45 22 99 12
		16 av de Friedland	
	Unilangues	61 bd Haussmann	42 68 04 02
	Institut Audio Visuel	40 rue de Berri	45 63 52 74
	Lingua Formation	61 rue d'Anjou	42 65 77 30
	OSFP Formation/		
	Dialangues	7 rue de Surène	42 68 18 54
	Southport Language Centre	74 rue du fg Saint Honoré	42 65 45 20
	CFL	12 rue Lincoln	42 25 48 83
	ADELE	1 rue de la Pépinière	
	Linguarama	5 rue Royale	42 65 18 47
9e	Stirling International	12 rue Hippolyte Lebas	45 26 25 21
	Transfer Formation Conseil	20 rue Godot de Mauroy	42 66 14 11

9e	Languacom	41 rue Chaussée d'Antin	42 82 00 44

10e	ACREA	26 bd de Strasbourg	42 41 83 00
	Business & Technical Languages	9 cité Paradis	45 23 54 54
	Europa Formation	107 bd de Magenta	42 85 22 41
	IGS International	12 rue Alexandre Parodi	
	StudyLang	94 rue Lafayette	42 46 03 52
	Cybèle Langues	12 bd Bonne Nouvelle	45 23 12 09
11e	FCLC	26 rue des Boulets	43 71 59 28
	Euro-Teclangues	48 bd Voltaire	43 57 56 13
15e	IFG Langues	37 quai de Grenelle	
	ILIC	12 rue Letellier	
	Language Plus Services	24/26 rue du Cotentin	43 35 24 71
16e	Polyphone Langues	7 av de la Grande Armée	45 00 78 57
	Lanser Language Services	44 rue Paul Valéry	45 00 04 73
17e	Cetradel Etoile	9 Av Mac-Mahon	43 80 34 41
	Inlingua	172 rue de Courcelles	47 63 89 72
	Langues et Entreprises	18 rue de Tilsit	46 22 69 71
18e	ELE Sandwich Method	25 rue Bandelique	42 64 76 24
	Anglo Executive	50 rue Hermel	42 51 21 13
19e	Universal Communications	52 rue de Flandre	40 35 07 80

Suburbs

Le Vesinet,78110
    AAA Business communications 21 route de la Croix   30 53 23 04
La Defense,92081

IFERP	Berkeley Building	47 76 41 76
Linguarama	Tour Eve	47 74 66 63

Courbevoie,92400

Langage Forum	20 place de l'Iris	47 73 57 28

Ivry-sur-Seine,94200

Télélangues Systèmes	9 rue Maurice Grandcoing	45 73 33 33

Neuilly,92200

Totale Formation	114 av de Charles	46 37 56 40

Further information:
Institutions offering English Languages Tuition in the Paris area,
The British Council, 9/11 rue de Constantine,75007 Paris

Bilingual Secretaries

Qualified bilingual secretaries can usually find a job reasonably quickly in Paris. Special attention should be paid to the contract, conditions of work, holidays and salary offered before signing on the dotted line. Sudden, unexplained, changes in work, hours and pay are not unknown. If this happens, write immediately to the *Ministère du Travail* (who should send an inspector) and send a copy of the letter to employer.

Experienced secretaries are relatively well paid. *Débutant(e)s* (first job) are not. *Débutant(e)s* earn a salary of only 7500-8500frs. However, debutant status only applies to the first six months of work. After that, employee is *expérimenté (e)* and can expect to be paid 9000-11000frs. General requirements are typing, shorthand (minimum 100wpm), word processing (almost essential now), good spoken French and some ability to type in French, and also to type from manuscript in English and French. A secretary may be asked to learn French shorthand.

Some agencies in Paris for bilingual secretaries

> **Kelly Girl** have several offices, the largest Tour Maine-Montparnasse 33 av du Maine 75015 tel 45 38 52 03 M° Monparnasse-Bienvenue/106bis rue St. Lazarre 75008 tel 42 93 20 20 M° St. Lazarre
> **Manpower**, 9 rue Jacques-Bingen, 75017 Paris, tel 47 66 03 03 M° Malesherbes
> **Minerve Interim**, 11 rue de Havre, 75008 Paris M° St Lazare tel 42 93 68 53
> **Randstad**, 20 rue Pierre Lescot, 75001 Paris, tel 42 33 61 01 M° Etienne Marcel
> **Ecco**, 90 rue Lafayette Paris 75009, tel 42 46 02 14 M° Poissonière.
> **G. R. Interim**, 12 rue de le Paix, 75002 Paris, tel 42 61 82 11 M° Opéra
> **Hôtesse Sécretaire S.A.**, 12 rue Chabanais, 75002 Paris, tel 42 96 34 80 / 42 61 81 03 M° Bourse.
> **Plus Interim**, 14 Place Denfert Rochereau, 75014 Paris, tel 43 22 47 22 M° Denfert Rochereau/ 14bis rue Marbeuf, 75008 Paris, tel 40 70 15 10 M° Franklin D. Roosevelt
> **Adia Interim**, 106ter rue St. Lazarre 75008 tel 42 93 50 02 M° St. Lazarre
> **Britt Travail Temporaire (Banking)**, 23 bd des Capucines, Paris 75002 tel 47 42 06 12 M° Opéra

Several international organisations are located in Paris. However, although the basic pay and conditions are very good, career opportunities are extremely limited. It is also becoming increasingly difficult to get permanent contracts in these organisations. The best time to apply is Spring/Summer before the holiday season starts. Write to the Head of Personnel at the following addresses:

Council of Europe, *(Conseil d'Europe)* 55 av Kléber,75016 Paris, tel 47 04 38 65 M° Kléber

European Space Agency (ESA), 8 rue Mario Nikis,75015 Paris, tel 42 73 76 54, M° Ségur

OECD /Organisation for Economic Co-operation and Development, 2 rue André-Pascal, 75775 Paris Cedex 16, tel 45 24 82 00 M° La Muette

UNESCO, Bureau of personnel recruitment unit, 7 Place de Fontenoy, 75007 Paris, tel 45 68 10 00 M° Ségur

Multinational companies also provide good hunting grounds:

Apple Computer Europe Inc., 80 av Président Wilson, 92800 Puteaux, tel 49 01 49 01, RER La Défense

Alcatel Trade International, 33 rue Emeriau,75015 Paris, tel 40 58 58 58 M° Charles Michels

Cleary, Gottlieb, Steen & Hamilton (Mme Féret), 41 av de Friedland, 75008 Paris, tel 40 74 68 00 M° Charles de Gaulle Etoile

Baker & McKenzie (Mme Nion), 67-69 av Victor Hugo, 75016 Paris, tel 44 17 53 00, M° Victor Hugo

Coopers & Lybrand, 59 rue Ponthieu, 75008 Paris, tel 44 20 80 00 M° Franklin D.Roosevelt

Frère Cholmeley, 42 av Président Wilson, 75016 Paris, tel 44 34 71 00 M° Iéna

IBM, 68 quai de la Rapée, 75012 Paris, tel 43 47 41 41 M° Bercy

IBM, 3 Place Vendôme, Paris 75001, tel 49 05 70 00 M° Opéra

IBM Europe, Tour Pascal, cedex 40, 92075 Paris,La Defense

International Herald Tribune, 181 av Charles de Gaulle, 92531 Neuilly, tel 46 37 93 00

Marks & Spencer, 35 bd Haussmann, 75009 Paris, tel 47 42 42 91 M° Havre-Caumartin

Price Waterhouse (Mme Picard), 18 Place Henri Bergson, 75008 Paris, tel 42 94 45 45 M° St-Augustin

H.S.D. Ernst & Young International, Tour Manhattan, 92092 Paris La Défense tel 46 93 60 00, RER La Défense

Sullivan & Cromwell, 8 Place Vendôme, Paris 75001, tel 42 60 02 35 M° Opéra

Davis Polk & Wardwell 4 Place de la Concorde, Paris 75008, tel 40 17 36 00 M° Concorde

Service

Euro Disneyland will open on 12 April 1992 but since the beginning of September 1991, it already began recruiting many of the 12,000 staff required including managers, secretaries, receptionists, hosts, waiters/waitresses etc, etc. In fact 1200 different roles require to be filled. 4000 will work in the theme park itself, 3000 others will work in the restaurants while another 1600 will organise entertainment in the hotels and other centres. Another 1000 will be required to maintain 5200 hotel rooms and 414 furnished bungalows. 11 million visitors are expected during the first year. Most of the staff will begin work in March but will be hired before that as they will be given special training. Disney's aim is to hire 70 people a day, six days a week up to March. Candidates should be out-going, social and good at communicating. Candidates are required to speak English and French though there are some posts which do not require a second language. As Disney is show business, it refers to casting rather than recruiting. The Casting Centre is open Mon-Sat, 9am-5pm at:

Le Vendôme III
11 rue du Rempart
Noisy-le-Grand

It is situated 32km east of Paris in Marne-la-Vallée and is accessible by RER, line A, direction Torcy - Marne-la-Vallée, station Noisy-le-Grand-Mont-d'Est, or by car, autoroute A4, sortie Noisy-le-Grand. It can be contacted also by Minitel, by dialing 3615 EURO DISNEY. Other recruiting centres have been opened in Holland, Germany and in Great Britain at:

1 Northumberland
London WC 2N4 BW
tel 872-5606, Fax 753-2765

Bureau de Change requires operatives, particularly in Summer. Wages are moderate and work uncomplicated.
Contact:
Bureau de Change, 52 av Champs Elysées, 75008 Paris,
tel 42 89 82 32/42 89 80 33 M° Franklin D. Roosevelt

Waiters/Waitresses New cafés, restaurants and bars (some Irish) open in Paris daily. A knowledge of restaurant, café or bar work can lead to many job opportunities for the right applicant. Wages are not high (4000 - 5500frs per month) but are augmented by tips.

Chambermaids are required in many large hotels, particularly in Summer when emigrant staff return home. Contact Holiday Inns or any of the other well-known chains.

Fast Food McDonald's,Freetime,etc are expanding rapidly all over Paris. Staff turnover is high. English-speaking staff are sought, particularly in Summer, to cater for American tourists. Wages are 30-40frs an hour, paid monthly into a bank account which must be opened for the purpose.

Supermarkets look for cashiers or *chef du rayon* (Head of Department). Wages run to about 6.000frs per month. Work permit *(carte de séjour)* is required (see Administration) Contracts are usually for a minimum of three months and should not be signed without careful study and a clear understanding of what is entailed.

Try M. Bergeot, Supermarché UNIMAG, 4-10 rue Dupleix, 75015 Paris,tel 47 34 31 23 (39 hours per week, Sunday plus one day free per week).

Société carrefour, Mme Sylvie Guy, Sunseil, Agence de Recruitment, 4-26 rue de Berri, 75008 Paris, tel 45 62 55 13 / 45 62 20 00 M° George V

A.N.P.E. *(Agence Nationale pour Emploi)*

This is the State Employment Agency which deals with about 20% of the jobs market in Paris. The only requirment is an E.E.C. passport. Job lists are posted on placards in the agency every morning. Note reference number and take it to desk person. Passport will be checked, prospective employer contacted and interview arranged. CV (in French) and references will help.

A.N.P.E.23 rue Taitbout, 75009 Paris, tel 42 46 92 47 M° Chaussée d'Antin
4 imp. d'Antin, 75008 Paris, tel 42 25 95 57 M° Champs Elysées
4 rue Simonet, 75013 Paris, tel 45 80 38 79 M° Corvisart
2 rue Crillon, 75004 Paris, tel 42 71 24 68 M° Arsenal
For others, consult telephone directory or Minitel.

Inspection du Travail

If terms or conditions of employment are sub-standard, contact the local *inspection du travail*. The local *mairie* will provide the address.

Further information:
Working in France (French Embassy,Dublin)

Voluntary Work

Voluntary work is available, particularly in Summer, but is recommended only for the highly-motivated.

Les Petits Frères des Pauvres are a lay organisation with a small permanent staff and a wide circle of volunteers *(bénévoles)* for the support of old people. During the year they visit old people in their homes to help with their practical needs and relieve their loneliness. In Summer they take them on holidays to the country. Volunteers help by cooking, cleaning, washing etc and spending time with the old. Volunteers must be over 18, speak French moderately well and be committed. They are provided with accommodation and food, travel expenses in (but not to) France and a small amount of pocket-money.
Contact *Les Petits Frères des Pauvres*, 64 av Parmentier, 75011 Paris, tel 47 00 75 55 M° Parmentier

l'Arche,founded by Jean Vanier to the help mentally handicapped, has more than 30 *foyers* in France including Paris. Assistants *(copains)* help by working and living with the handicapped. Work includes cooking and cleaning, gardening, making pottery or furniture in the workshops *(ateliers)*. Community and prayer life are central. French is recommended but not essential. Assistants work 6 days a week

with one weekend off per month. The first month is voluntary, with 450frs a month thereafter in addition to food and accommodation.
Contact *l'Arche*, La Ferme 25 route d'Orléans BP 35 Trosly, 6350 Cuise-la-motte tel 44 85 61 02

Les Orphelins Apprentis d'Auteuil, in the care of the French Holy Ghost Fathers *(les Spiritains)*, run 28 residencies, schools and training centers for young people in difficulty. In Summer they organise different holiday centers around France on the same lines as 'the Sunshine Homes' in Ireland. Irish volunteers are welcome. Some knowledge of French is required and an ability to work with young people from 'problem' families. Food, accommodation and pocket money is provided but not travel fare from Ireland.
Contact P. Gabriel David C.S.Sp. 40 rue de la Fontaine, 75761 Paris Cedex 16 tel 45 29 95 20 (before mid-Feb)

Useful Terminology

agence - agency
bilingue - bilingual
chef du rayon - head of department
débutante(e) - beginner
emploi - employment
employé(e) - employee
employeur - employer
expérimenté(e) - experienced
femme de chambre - chambermaid
garçon - waiter
gérant - manager
hôtesse - receptionist
rémunération - pay
salaire - salary
secrétaire - secretary
serveuse - waitress

Students

French Language Courses

Sorbonne: *Cours de civilisation française,* Galerie Richelieu de la Sorbonne, 47 rue des Ecoles, 75005, tel 40 46 22 11, ext. 2664 and 2675. RER Luxembourg/St. Michel.

Summer courses are held in June, July, August and September and are of varying lengths - 4, 6, 8 or 11 weeks. - depending on the type of course taken. Special courses, such as business French, are offered as well.

The Winter term is made up of two 12-week semesters, with one week for exams. Prices range from 4,300-9,500frs for Winter courses and Summer courses are about 2.000frs. To take a course, a Leaving Certificate level of French is usually required, except courses for beginners.

Alliance Française, 101 Boulevard Raspail, 75006 Paris, tel 45 44 38 28 M° Raspail

Offers evening and day courses all year round in written French and conversation, at all levels. It also offers special courses, e.g. business French. Courses start every month and usually run for four weeks; it is possible to attend half a session.

Classes are of 3 hours 30 minutes, 1 hour 45 minutes or 1 hour 30 minutes and cost 2,100frs, 1,050frs and 920frs per session respectively. There is also a registration fee of 180frs.

Institut Catholique de Paris, *Institut de langue et de culture françaises*, 21 rue d'Assas, 75006 Paris, tel 42 22 41 80 ext. 380/381 M° Rennes

Courses for beginners run from October-February and February-June and consist of 6 or 12 hours weekly for 15 weeks. Prices range from 2,900-7,300frs.

Mairie (Town Hall): Each *arrondissement* has its own *Mairie*, check the address in the telephone directory or at the post office.

The *Mairie* offers courses costing about 250frs per term. Courses usually begin in October and end in June. There are usually 30-40 students in each class.

Ecole Etoile, 4 place Saint-Germain-des-Prés, 75006 Paris, tel 45 48 00 05, M° Saint-Germain-des-Prés.
Courses run from 1 October to the end of June. Also possible to join at the beginning of each month if there are places available. Courses consist of 5 two-hour sessions per week, mornings or afternoons.

Ecole France Langue, 2 rue de Sfax, 95116 Paris, tel 45 00 40 15, M° Victor Hugo
Courses run from 30 September to 26 June. 3-month session costs 14,940frs plus 180frs enrollment fee. One week (30hrs) costs 1,660frs and two weeks (15hrs) costs 1,660frs.

Eurocentre, 13.1 passage Dauphine, 75006 Paris, tel 43 25 81 40, M° Saint Michel
Intensive courses, 4 weeks, long courses, 12-14 weeks, with 20-30 lessons per week, from 30 September to April. Costs 1525frs per week (intensive), and 1400frs (long).

Institut Europeen de Langues et de Communication, 20-22 rue Richer, 75009 Paris, tel 45 23 35 70, M° Cadet
750frs per month for 2 hrs per day (10 hrs per week)

Accord, 72 rue Rambuteau, 75001 Paris, tel 42 36 24 95, M° Rambuteau
20 hrs per week for 4 weeks, 2000frs: 10 hrs a week for 4 weeks, 1300frs, 3 hrs a week for 4 weeks, 600frs.

Institut de Langue Française, 15 rue Arsène Houssaye, 75008 Paris, tel 42 27 14 77, M° Etoile
Language courses 6,10, 20 hrs per week. Special *au pair* /student price for 6 hr week, 1700frs per trimester

Institut Parisien de Langue et de Civilization Françaises, 87 bd de Grenelle, 75015 Paris, tel 40 56 09 53, M° La Motte Picquet
For 15 hrs per week, 1950frs for 4 weeks, 2700frs for 6 weeks. For 25 hrs per week, 3250frs for 4 weeks, 4500frs for 6 weeks.

C.I.E.L.F., 15 rue d'Hauteville, 75010 Paris, tel 48 00 06 93, M° Bonne Nouvelle
Intensive, 3 month, and evening courses

Further information:
Cours de français langue étrangère *(Ministère des Affairs étrangères)*

Libraries

Bibliotheque Nationale, 58 rue Richelieu, 75008 Paris
M° Palais-Royal

First get a reader's card.
Carte annuelle 140frs
Demi-tarif (for *boursiers* and *invités* of French govt.*)*
70frs
Carte de 8 entrées
30frs
Demi-tarif (à justifier)
35frs
Carte de 8 entrées
30frs

Undergraduates can usually only be granted a *carte de 8 entrées,* on condition that they present a letter of introduction. Go in person to the *services d'accueil* in the entrance hall, explain research project and the nature of the material to be consulted, produce a *pièce d'identité* and photos.

Specialized sections:
Imprimés: The printed book section, consisting of the main reading room, the catalogue room, and access to the Reserve. To consult a book in the main reading room go to *contrôle* with your reader's card and take a seat at the number allocated. Present reader's card and the *plaque* with seat number at the *bureau central* . Complete a docket for the book(s) required. Dockets are available at strategic points of the reading room and in the catalogue room (green for seats on right hand side, and white for left hand side of reading-room). Fill in seat number, Paris address, and book shelf number. The shelf number of the required book may be found in the catalogue room; situated on the floor below (accessible only from the reading room). Deliver completed docket(s) (maximum of ten a day) at the mail chute at *bureau central*. Book(s) will be delivered in about 35 minutes.

While waiting for the book(s) to arrive, investigate the shelves, surrounding the reading room; they contain not only dictionaries and encyclopedias of all sorts, biographical, etymological, and theological, and other standard *usuels*, but the best-known definitive editions of all the major writers of the West from Aristotle to Zola - all on ready reference.

*Périodiques:*Theperiodicalssectionisalsohuge,containinganimmense range of journals and newspapers; for all but a number of special titles (available on microfilm), publications dating from before 1950 must be consulted at the *annexe* in Versailles. The *salle des périodiques* is on the ground floor behind the main staircase.

Manuscrits: The manuscripts library appears to hold every document ever drafted by anyone who ever held office in France. If the document sought is not available here, the catalogues of the ms. room will help to find it. First find the appropriate catalogue inventory. Librarians and *conservateurs* on the central desk are very knowledgeable, and are there to help. The manuscripts room is on the second floor of the library, at the head of the main staircase.

Estampes: The collection of prints of the B. N. includes work by artists such as Bosse, Callot, Matisse, Picasso, Van Dyck, Rubens and Dürer, etc. The shelf numbers of collections of prints available for consultation are to be found in the catalogues which line the right hand wall of the room. It is possible, on completion of the appropriate order form, to have the prints reproduced by the B. N. photographic services. Where the print concerned has already been reproduced, a *cliché* is kept in the series of *cliché* files where it can be consulted. Reproduction from an extant negative is much cheaper than the usual cost.

Note: A reader's card for the Bibliothèque Nationale gains admission to any other state library in France.

L'Arsenal 1 rue de Sully, 75004 Paris M° Sully-Morland; a specialised annex of the B. N. and it is free. It has been developed as the national library of theatre studies, *La Bibliothèque des Arts du Spectacle* (which includes dance, design and cinema); it also has particularly rich collections of medieval and early modern manuscripts, and an outstanding collection of prints and drawings. Two important twentieth century bequests, by Auguste Rondel and Louis Jouvet, have confirmed and concentrated the strength of the library as a centre for drama studies. The library is on the first floor of the building, at the head of the marble staircase. The staff are very friendly. Ask for a reader's card (with a *pièce d'identité*), at the reception desk.

Bibliotheque Ste- Genevieve Place du Panthéon, 75005 Paris, RER Luxembourg. Magnetic readers' cards are delivered on request, and free, in the reception area of the main hall. This gives access to the reading room on the floor above. The collections of the library are extremely rich, most material relating to the history and literature of France can be found here. A further asset is that photocopying, in contrast to the B. N., is not only much easier here, but much cheaper (1fr a double page). The catalogue and reference rooms, which are much easier to use than those of the B. N., are across the *passerelle* behind the main reading-room (also surrounded with ready reference *usuels*). On the ground floor of the library, opposite the readers' services, (and in the same building) is the entrance to the *bibliothèque Jacques Doucet* and the manuscript collections. The Jacques Doucet Library specialises in literary manuscript material, especially modern poetry. There is a number of seventeenth-century Irish documents here.

Bibliotheque de La Sorbonne is to be avoided. The services are overstretched and undermanned.

Bibliotheque du Centre Pompidou 75003 Paris M° Rambuteau, is designed as the modern reference library (and art gallery and conference centre) for the next century,equipped with all available gadgetry. There are art galleries, the art shop and *carterie*, the fabulous view of Paris from the top floor (access free on the escalator), and all the fun of the entertainers, fire-eaters and sword-swallowers, who regularly perform in the open space outside the centre. No entry requirements for the library.

B.D.I.C., Nanterre *Bibliothèque de la Documentation Internationale Contemporaine,* at the University of Nanterre RER Nanterre-Université. One of the most useful, friendly, and underrated libraries in the Paris region. It holds much of central importance to students of politics, economics and modern history. The range of material covers topics such as colonialism and decolonisation (especially French Empire), Eastern European alignments, Third World development, terrorist movements, and military miscellanea; the material is very often photocopied from originals in Africa, Asia, or ex-Iron Curtain countries. The centre is on the ground floor of the tower which stands on the main Nanterre campus, a few hundred yards from the R.E.R. station, and across the university tennis courts and running track. Reader's card is issued free and for life, on presentation of *pièce d'identité* and photos.

Bibliotheque Historique de la Ville de Paris Situated in the Hôtel Lamoignon in the *quartier du Marais,* 24, rue Pavée, 75004 Paris, tel 42 74 44 44 M° St.Paul. Specialises, in the history of Paris. Informal and uncomplicated registration procedure, with catalogues which are easy to consult. Open Monday - Saturday 9.30am - 6pm.

Bibliotheque Administrative de L'Hotel De Ville 75004 Paris, tel 42 76 48 87 M° Hôtel de Ville. It is in the building of the Hôtel de Ville, staircase W, 5th floor, specialising in the administrative affairs of the capital and of the former department of the Seine, and also includes some overseas material; could usefully replace the need to consult *Archives de Paris.*

Bibliotheque Marguerite Durand 79, rue Nationale, 75013, Paris, tel 45 70 80 30 M° Nationale or Tolbiac. Specialises in women's affairs and the history of the feminist movement.

Bibliotheque Forney, Hôtel de Sens, rue du Figuier, 75004 Paris, tel 42 78 14 60 M° Pont Marie. Specialises in the decorative arts.

Bibliotheque des Arts Graphiques 78 rue Bonaparte, 75006 Paris, tel 43 54 88 78 M° St Sulpice. Specialises in history and illustration of the book, and techniques of printing.

Discotheque des Halles Situated at the Forum des Halles, 8 porte St Eustache, 75001 Paris, tel 42 33 20 50 M° Châtelet, and is for music appreciation and access to sound archives; records may, on specific conditions, be borrowed.

Bibliotheques D'Arrondissement To get a reader's card it is necessary to have a letter of introduction from *proprietaire* showing *bona fide* residency in Paris (at least 6 months) and *pièce d'identité*. *Bibliothèques d'arrondissement* are well stocked with reference books, periodicals, current fiction, and *grands auteurs* and allow borrowing several books/periodicals for up to a fortnight. Some have record lending libraries, and others specialise in particular themes (crime writing in 5th arrondissement, Mouffetard-Contrescarpe; cinema in the 6th arrondissement, André Malraux; musical scores in the 12th arrondissement, Picpus; tourism and sport in the 16th, Trocadéro).

The Libraries are open all year from Tuesday to Saturday.

Note: Local library is an unrivalled source of information for cultural events in the neighbourhood.

Municipal libraries

There are 59 municipal libraries and the following is a complete list of those for adults:

1er	Mairie, 4 rue du Louvre	tel 42 60 05 65 M° Louvre
2e	2 passage des Petits-Pères	tel 42 96 45 98 M° Bourse
3e	Mairie, 2 rue Eugene-Spuller	tel 42 72 90 70 M° Temple
4e	Mairie, 2 place Baudoyer	tel 48 8749 88 M° Hôtel de Ville
5e	74-76 rue Mouffetard	tel 43 37 96 54 M° Monge
	15bis rue Buffon	tel 45 87 12 27 M° Gare d'Austerlitz
	88ter bd de Port-Royal	tel 43 25 74 16 RER Port Royal
6e	78 bd Raspail (André Malraux)	tel 45 44 53 85 M° Rennes

7e	Mairie, 116 rue de Grenelle	tel 47 05 43 73 M° Varenne
	164 rue de Grenelle	tel 47 05 89 66 M° Latour - Maubourg
8e	Mairie, 3 rue de Lisbonne	tel 45 22 86 52 M° Europe
9e	24 rue de Rochechouart	tel 42 85 27 56 M° Cadet
10e	81 bd de la Villette	tel 42 41 14 30 M° Colonel Fabien
	Mairie, 72 rue du Faubourg St Martin	tel 42 40 10 10 M° Chateau d'Eau
11e	18-20 rue Faidherbe	tel 43 71 71 16 M° Faidherbe Chaligny
12e	70 rue de Picpus	tel 43 45 87 12 M° Bel Air
	23 rue du Colonel Rozanoff	tel 43 45 68 86 M° Diderot
13e	211-13 bd Vincent Auriol	tel 45 80 21 75 M° Place d'Italie
	132 rue de la Glacière	tel 45 89 55 47 M° Glacière
14e	26 rue Mouton-Duvernet	tel 45 39 34 88 M° Mouton-Duvernet
	5 rue de Ridder	tel 45 41 24 74 M° Plaisance
	80 av du Maine	tel 43 22 42 18 M° Gaité
15e	36-40 rue Emeriau	tel 45 77 63 40 M° Charles Michels, Dupleix
	154 rue Lecourbe	tel 48 28 77 42 M° Vaugirard
16e	6 rue du Commandant-Schloesing	tel 47 04 70 85 M° Trocadéro
	20 rue de Musset	tel 45 25 69 83 M° Chardon-Lagache
17e	11 rue Jacques Bingen	tel 47 63 03 25 M° Malesherbes
	Mairie, 18 rue des Batignolles	tel 42 93 35 17 M° Clichy
18e	29 rue Hermel	tel 42 54 13 93 M° Jules Joffrin
	18 av de la Porte Montmartre	tel 42 55 60 20 M° Porte de Clignancourt
	8 rue Pierre Budin	tel 42 54 11 42 M° Marcadet-Poissonniers
19e	18 rue Janssen	tel 42 49 55 90 M° Pré Saint-Gervais
	34-5 rue de Flandre	tel 40 35 96 46 M° Riquet
	6 rue Fessart	tel 42 08 49 15 M° Jourdain
20e	37-9 rue St Blaise	tel 43 67 77 61 M° Porte de Bagnolet
	12 rue du Télégraphe	tel 43 66 84 29 M° Télégraphe
	66 rue des Couronnes	tel 47 97 80 84 M° Couronnes

Further information:

Annuaire des Bibliothèques and
Guide des Bibliothèques et Discothèques de la Ville de Paris
(Mairie de Paris, Direction des Affaires Culturelles) in local library.

Archives

The archival wealth of Paris is enormous. While some Irish researchers have non-Irish interests, a particular feature is the amount of documentation on the Irish who served in Ancien Régime France. For most archives, the initial visit, an identity document (passport for foreigners) plus two photographs is required. In addition, the Archives du Ministère des Affaires Etrangères will require a letter of recommendation from either a French research supervisor or from the Irish Embassy. Visitors on a flying visit should allow for a good deal of time being taken up with formalities on the first visit. It can be useful to write in advance setting out the object of the research, as the reply can be helpful in varying degrees. Archives are closed, apart from public holidays, for a short period each year and it is advisable to ascertain this before planning a visit to Paris.

Archives Nationales, 11, rue des Quatre-Fils, 75003 Paris, tel 40 27 64 19 M° Ramuteau. Magnetic card issued with photo taken on the spot and yearly card costs 100frs. Insert card to open the doors of the *salle des inventaires* and *salle de lecture*. In the reading room ask for a place number. Then use the magnetic card in computer terminals for ordering documents. The staff will assist but the system is easily mastered. Five cartons may be consulted each day. It is also possible to reserve cartons *en prolongation* for another day. Documents may also be reserved for a future date. All reservations must be made at the latest before 4pm on the day before consultation and before 6pm for a later date and the documents are held in reservation for a week. Documents may also be reserved from home by using the Minitel and dialling 3616 CARAN after 7pm. Photocopying facilities are available in a room adjacent to the reading room from 9.15am-5.15pm. Beforehand, the permission of the president must be sought. Tickets may be bought in books of different quantities at the reception on the ground floor and one ticket pays for each page photocopied. The archives are open Mon-Sat, 9am-6pm all year round (except for 2 weeks after 14 July and public holidays). NB Documents must be ordered in advance for Saturdays when photocopying facilities finish at 1.15pm.

Archives de la Guerre Chateau de Vincennes, Paris, tel 49 57 32 00, *poste* 24 33 M° Chateau de Vincennes. This archive is equipped with a large collection of officer, rank and file lists and miltary correspondence. It has a lot of material of Irish interest and the published catalogues are helpful, especially the correspondence of the Ancien Régime. Open Mon-Fri, 9 am to 5pm. Bring *pièce d'identité*.

Archives de Paris 18 Bd. Sérurier, 75019 Paris tel 42 39 55 55 M° Porte des Lilas. Open Monday 2-5:20pm, Tues-Fri 9:20am to 5:20pm, Sat 9:30am to 4:50pm, (except first 2 weeks in August, Saturdays in July and August and public holidays).On Saturdays only documents reserved at the latest before 4pm on the previous Wednesday may be consulted. Documents may be consulted by filling out a slip *(bulletins)*. These are attended to *(levées de bulletins)* every half-hour until 4.15pm. Bring a photo and *pièce d'Identité*.

Archives des Affaires Etrangeres 37 Quai d'Orsay, 75007 Paris, M° Invalides. Letter required from Embassy, stating qualifications and nature and purpose of research. Write ahead to insure acceptance and issue of reader's card. Bring a photo and *pièce d'Identité*.

Archives de la Prefecture de la Police 4 rue Montagne-Ste-Geneviève, 75005 Paris, tel 43 29 21 57 M° Maubert-Mutualité. Access is easy and free. Show *pièce d'identité* to policeman on duty. Ask for archives at *bureau d'accueil*. It is on the third floor through door marked Musée. Open Mon- Fri until 5pm.

Archives Departementales des Yvelines, Versailles Grands Ecuries du Roi, 1 av de Paris, 78000 Versailles, tel 39 02 78 78 *postes* 33 01, 33 08. Open Mondays, 12.30-5.30pm, Tues-Fri, 9am-5.30pm. *Levés les bulletins* every 45 mins from 9.30-11am and from 1-4.30pm. RER line C from Paris to Versailles Rive Gauche, 12frs, 40 mins. Bring photo and *pièce d'identité*.

Musee Carnavalet 23 rue de Sevigne, 75003 Paris M° Saint-Paul. Holds good collection of historical prints of Paris. Entry free. No card required.

Further information:
I'm going to France. A Guide for Foreign Students *(Centre National des Oeuvres Universitaires et Scolaires.)*

Bureaucracy

Residence Permit and Work Papers *(Carte de séjour, Carte de travail)*

Requirements:
- two letters from employer called *contrat d'engagement* are required stating length of contract, qualifications, working hours, etc.
- Four photographs, passport and three photocopies of passport. Photographs must be black and white in the case of EC nationals.
-A receipt for the rent *(quittance de loyer)*, gas (GdF) or electricity (EdF) bills as proof of living in France (or an *attestation de domicile* from the head of foyer).
-A stamped adressed envelope.

EC nationals should present above to Préfecture de Police (Section CEE), 93 av Parmentier, 75011 Paris M° Parmentier

A *carte de séjour* entitles the holder to work in France for periods of two years, five years or ten years as indicated by the official stamp on the card. It is also an official residence permit and must be carried always, to produce to police, in shops, etc as a *pièce d'identité*. If a change of address occurs (e.g. leaving the Paris area etc.), the *carte de séjour* must be adjusted at the local Préfecture. To renew the *carte de séjour* return to the Préfecture at least one month before the expiration date. Bring a stamped addressed envelope, the old *carte de séjour/travail*, gas or electricity bill, four photographs, and a letter from your employer stating initial date of employment, qualifications, working hours, monthly salary and social advantages.

Consular services

Passports
For first issue the applicant must submit:
a) his/her Irish birth certificate
b) completed PAS form,
c) two certified photographs, and
d) the required fee (320frs at present).

In order to have a passport with expired validity replaced, the applicant must submit:
a) the expired passport,
b) a completed PAS form, and
c) two certified photographs.

For persons under 18 years the written witnessed consent of both parents is necessary before a passport can be issued. The names of children can be added to the passport of a parent provided the written witnessed consent of the other parent is submitted. Children can be issued with a passport in their own name from birth.

Persons who lose their passports while in France should
a) notify the local police,
b) get a statement from the police to this effect.
The Embassy can issue either an emergency passport for travel to Ireland or a replacement passport to persons who either live abroad or who need to travel.

Applicants for emergency passports should submit proof of identity, two photographs and a copy of the police report concerning the loss/theft of their passport. The application forms are available at the Embassy.

Fiche d'Etat Civil

The Embassy can issue this document to holders of an Irish birth certificate. The applicants must produce the original full version (version giving parents' names) of the birth certificate and their passport.

The *Fiche d'Etat Civil* is, in some cases, accepted by the French authorities as the equivalent of a French translation of the birth certificate. It is asked for by the French authorities for the issue of documents such as the *carte de séjour* (residence permit), the social security card and number, and for a variety of things such as registering children at school, applying for children's allowances, etc.

However, the *fiche* is not acceptable to the French authorities for services such as marriage, most legal procedures, applications for certificate of character, etc. The applicant must find out from the relevant French authority whether or not the *fiche* is acceptable for the service he/she is applying for.

Certificat de Coutume

Irish persons who wish to get married in France will need to produce a *Certificat de Coutume et de Célibat* to the Mairie (Town Hall). The Embassy issues this document. The applicant must submit a completed questionnaire and a sworn declaration (the sworn declaration may be made at the Embassy when convenient to the applicant), his/her full version of the original birth certificate and their Irish passport.

Advance of Funds

The Embassy can assist persons whose money (or travel tickets) are either lost or stolen in France to have money transferred from Ireland to France to enable such persons to return home.

Before travelling abroad you should take out adequate insurance to cover against accident, illness or loss of possessions. The Embassy does not have funds to help citizens in need.

The necessary forms for the above transactions are available at the Embassy.

In some cases the Embassy can take sworn affidavits in English for use in the Irish legal system. Persons wishing to make affidavits at the Embassy should be in possesssion of an identity document such as a passport. Prior appointment is necessary.

Note: Irish citizens coming to France for the first time are advised to bring the original of any document they intend using in France. Photocopies of documents are not acceptable either to the French authorities or to the Embassy.

Legal Advice

Each year the *Ordre des Avocats à la Cour de Paris* publishes a directory of lawyers in Paris, entitled *Avocats à la Cour de Paris,* in which lawyers are classified according to their fields of expertise and language ability. English-speaking lawyers are listed. A copy of the directory may be consulted in the Irish Embassy.

Free Legal Advice/Assistance
Those unable to afford the services of a lawyer should contact an *assistante sociale* in local *mairie*. Please note however that legal aid is subject to a strict means test and is normally available to those with an established right of residence in France.

Notaries

Those requiring the services of a notary (equivalent to an Irish Commissioner for Oaths) should consult a directory of notaries at the Irish Embassy. The directory classifies them according to their fields of expertise and language ability.

Driving Licences

As EC nationals, Irish citizens are required to exchange their Irish driving licences for the French equivalent within one year of taking up residence in France. The following equivalence operates between Irish and French categories:

Irish	French
A	A
B	*tracteurs agricoles*
C	B
D	C

Missing Persons

If friend or relative goes missing in France their absence should be reported to the *Commissariat de Police* of the district where they were last seen. A central police unit for the Paris area (*Délégation Judiciaire*) tel 45 82 91 91, registers all such enquiries and if the person is still missing after 24 hrs, initiates an investigation into their whereabouts. For information regarding persons who may have been hospitalized, call *Centre de Renseignements Hospitaliers* tel 40 27 30 00 during office hours Mon-Fri.

Income Tax *(Impôts sur les Revenues) (Impôts Revenues Personne Physique - IRPP)*

Everyone is obliged to provide annually (in April) a statement of income for the preceeding year. A special form supplied by the IRPP Administration Office is used. This declaration should be returned to the *Contrôleur des Contributions* at the local *Mairie* (town hall).

New salaried workers do not pay tax during their first year of work in France. This does not mean that they are exempt from taxation. They pay in full the following August and their first tax bill is usually hefty. Hence long-term provision should be made for this. The ceiling below which one does not pay taxes changes slightly every year. This ceiling is referred to as the SMIC *(Salaire Minimum Interprofessionnel de Croissance)* On 1 December 1990 the SMIC was 5,397.88frs. Workers earning this sum or less were not taxed. Variations in the SMIC are linked to variations in the rate of inflation etc. It is advisable to check with the local *Trésor Public* (Tax/Revenue office) for the precise annual ceiling.

Payment: After the second year, there are two possibilities:
-To pay monthly by bank transfer to the *Trésor Public;*
-To pay in three instalments as follows:
a) before 15th February - one third of total tax for previous year;
b) before 15th May - one third of the total tax for previous year;
c) the remaining amount is paid when the official note is received (i.e. anytime after the beginning of August.)
NB: French tax forms are confusing and advice should be sought from employer's Business Office or any accountant *(comptable)*

Paid vacation trip

All salaried people have the right once a year to a return trip ticket on the SNCF with a reduction of 30% for a distance of 200kms. The spouse and children may also benefit from this reduction. The request should be presented at a railway station at least 48 hours before the date of departure and the necessary forms filled out.

Pay slips *(Feuille de paie)*

All pay slips should be carefully kept. They could be requested for inspection or verification by certain administrative departments. They are indispensable in order to be reimbursed by social security (if one does not have an annual statement). Pay slips can also be used to justify the total of salaries received at the time of retirement or of departure.

Continuous Professional Training *(Formation Professionnelle)*

A law enacted in 1971 provides for the continuous professional training of people throughout their working life and allows them, whether employed or unemployed, to acquire a skill, to improve their skills or to adapt to new skills made necessary by technological progress.

Conditions:
- Salaried people have a right to apply for a leave of absence to follow an approved training programme, if they have been employed for at least two years. However, a request may be refused if, (i) the funds are not available; (ii) it disorganises a department.

- People with higher degrees or with professional degrees/diplomas acquired less than three years previously are excluded.

- An employer can postpone leave of absence applications so that no more than 2% of of the work force would be on leave at the same time.

- The maximum leave of absence is one year on a full time basis or 1200 hours on a part time basis, with a few exceptions.

Banking

All EC nationals may open either a *Compte Etranger en France* or a *Compte de Résident*. The main difference between the two is that the *Compte Etranger* is not subject to currency controls. Please note that overdrafts, no matter how small are not allowed. French banks take this rule very seriously and any slip-up may result in cheque book *(chequier)* and/or credit cards being confiscated (for a minimum of a year). Some banks also stipulate a minimum balance (e.g. 100frs) on current accounts.

Opening a bank account requires:
- a valid passport or *carte de séjour*,
- proof of residence (electricity, telephone or rent bill, showing

clearly present address. For those in *foyers* or hostels an *attestation de domicile* signed by the head usually suffices.

- the newly-arrived should request written confirmation from employer of contract of employment to use as proof of financial status. (They may also arrange to have salaries paid direct into bank accounts).

NB: Change money in a bank rather than in Bureau de Change. It costs less. Check bank charges, especially when changing small amounts.

Useful Terminology

attestation de domicile - certificate of residence
carte de séjour - resident's permit
chequier - cheque book
compte étranger - foreign account
compte de résident - resident's account
contrat d'engagement - work contract
feuille de paie - pay slip
impôt sur les revenues - income tax
quittance de loyer - rent receipt
trésor public - tax/revenue office

Communication

Telephone

There are two types of public telephones; those that accept coins and those that accept cards.

Coin Phones accept coins from 1- 5frs. The minimum charge is 1fr to place a call anywhere, which allows 19 seconds during reduced rate periods for EC countries. Give the number of the cabin to be called back if short of cash. 20frs will allow six and a half minutes during reduced rate periods.

For assistance in finding telephone numbers dial 12.

Card Phones can be purchased at any post office or *Tabac*. They come in two varieties: 50 units costing 40frs and 120 units costing 96frs. Units are used progressively until the card is finished. There is no financial advantage/disadvantage in using cards. However, they are often easier to find and practical for long distance calls. Card phones are becoming increasingly more widespread than coin phones.

Those who have a private phone can apply for a *Carte Pastel*. It is valid for 1 year and all calls made using it are charged to the telephone bill. The Pastel card can be used to telephone from countries outside France and again with the charge being billed directly to your account. It is useful for those who use public phones or travel a lot. It has a secret code which prevents non- authorised use if it happens to be lost or stolen. In addition, it can be used in coin operated phones by dialling 3650 and supplying the secret code. If the phone is connected to a digital centre (usually phones with keypads), dial 3610 and input the code directly. The Pastel card is as easy to use as the classic phone cards but even more flexible and doesn't run out of units. It costs 80frs per year for an international card and 65frs per year for a national (France only). It can be requested at local PTT agency.

Private Phones

For a private phone go to the local PTT agency. (to find dial 14 from a local phone). Show an EDF (electricity) bill or a rental receipt *(quittance de loyer)* as proof of residence and some form of identification e.g. passport. Connection usually takes a short time (1-2 weeks) and you can normally choose the phoneset. Be careful as the more sophisticated sets have a higher monthly charge.

Acquire a minitel instead of a paper phone directory. This is useful as it contains all French telephone numbers. (Directory only gives regional numbers).

Many other services are offered but usually mean paying an extra subscription. The most interesting is probably the possibility of having a detailed breakdown of the telephone bill. This is useful if sharing an apartment with others. It could be useful to avoid arguments about who is calling home most! This service costs 8frs per month for up to 100 calls and 10frs a month for each additional 100 calls.

For a wake-up call telephone the operator or with a touch phone (i.e. keypad) press *55*HHMM# where HHMM is the time using a 24 hour clock. E.g. *55*0715# would place a wakeup call for 7.15am. To verify correct input press *#55*HHMM#. To cancel a call press #55*HHMM#. A busy signal indicates that the number has been input incorrectly and a dial tone at the end of the operation tells you that you have been successful. This service costs 3.65frs per call.

Other interesting features are the ability to take a second call while talking to another caller and transferring calls to an external number. This could be useful if expecting an important call but need to go somewhere else for the evening, weekend, etc. Details of these and other services can be obtained from local PTT agency.

You can ask to be excluded from the telephone directory (both paper and minitel) but this service will cost you 15frs per month. Just ask to be put on the *Liste Rouge*.

Most of these services require electronic exchanges which are progressively being introduced all over France.

Minitel

A minitel gives access to many services in France, e.g. to find a telephone number. Numbers can be searched by name or by category. Categories can be doctors, hotels, restaurants, etc., e.g. list of doctors in locality. Minitel is provided free for the basic model (though sometimes difficult to get) and up to 230frs per month for the most sophisticated models with built in phone.

To operate a minitel, make sure that it is plugged into the phone socket with the telephone plugged into it. Switch on the minitel. Lift the phone and dial 11. When you hear a high pitch whistle, press *Connexion/Fin* to establish the connection. Replace the telephone as if hanging up. A page of information should appear on the screen of the minitel. Type in the surname after the word *NOM* using the keypad on the minitel. Now press *Suite* and the small white square will move to the next line labelled *RUBRIQUE*. Type in the type of service required in French e.g. *DENTISTE* for a list of dentists or *RESTAURANT* for a list of restaurants. (Type something for either the name *(NOM)* or the service *(RUBRIQUE)* to make a valid request. Press *Suite* to continue. On the line marked *LOCALITÉ* type the name of the town where the person/service is (e.g. Paris or 75015 for the 15th *arrondissement)*. This is optional. Press *Suite* to go to the next line. Enter the *Département* number/name that you wish to search.

If a mistake is made press *Retour* to return to the previous line. Finally press ENVOI. After a short pause, the minitel will print a list of names and associated telephone numbers. The first 3 minutes are free and it costs 40 centimes for each minute after. To terminate, press *Connexion/Fin* and switch off minitel.

Many other services can be accessed by the minitel by dialling 36 14, 36 15 or 36 16. To find a list of the services available dial 36 14 and type MGS. This will give a list of themes and associated services. Be wary when connected to 36 14, 36 15 or 36 16. It costs per minute and telephone bill mounts rapidly.

Call Rates
Call charging is divided into two areas: France (including overseas departments) and international calls. Call charges are as follows for France:Minitel

		Public Phone		Private Phone	
Mon - Fri:	Rate/10 mins.	Local	Over 100km	Local	Over 100km
6 - 8am	50% reduction	0.63frs	15frs	0.60frs	13.7frs
8 -12:30am	Full charge	1.25frs	30frs	1.20frs	27.3frs
12:30am-13:30pm	30% reduction	0.88frs	21frs	0.84frs	19.11frs
13:30 -18pm	Full charge	1.25frs	30frs	1.20frs	27.3frs
18 -21:30pm	30% reduction	0.88frs	21frs	0.84frs	19.11frs
21:30-22:30pm	50% reduction	0.63frs	15frs	0.60frs	13.7frs
22:30pm-6am	65% reduction	0.44frs	10.5frs	0.42frs	9.55frs

		Public Phone		Private Phone	
Saturday:	Rate/10 mins.	Local	Over 100km	Local	Over 100km
6-8am	50% reduction	0.63frs	15frs	0.60frs	13.7frs
8-12:30am	Full charge	1.25frs	30frs	1.20frs	27.3frs
12:30am-13:30pm	30% reduction	0.88frs	21frs	0.84frs	19.11frs
13:30-22:30pm	50% reduction	0.63frs	15frs	0.60frs	13.7frs
22:30pm-6am	65% reduction	0.44frs	10.5frs	0.42frs	9.55frs

Sun/ holidays	Rate/10 mins.	Local	Over 100km	Local	Over 100km
6am-22:30pm	50% reduction	0.63frs	15frs	0.60frs	13.7frs
22:30pm-6am	65% reduction	0.44frs	10.5frs	0.42frs	9.55frs

Europe

Mon- Fri:	Rate/10mins	Charge
8am-21.30pm	Full charge	45frs
21.30pm-8am	2/3 normal price	30.4frs

Saturday:	Rate/10mins	Charge
8am-14pm	Full charge	45frs
14pm-8am	2/3 normal price	30.4frs

Sun/ holidays	Rate/10mins	Charge
All day	2/3 normal price	30.4frs

Postal information

Letters

Letters must not be over 5kg.
Rates for France and EC countries are the following:

Up to	20g	2.50frs	50g	4.00frs
	100g	6.20frs	250g	11frs
	500g	15frs	1000g	20frs
	2000g	27frs	3000g	32frs
	5000g	38frs		

Parcels

Parcels must weigh less than 7kg and not be longer than 60cm. The three dimensions when added together should not exceed 100cm. Boxes are sold in the post office to send parcels.

Collisimo is a service which ensures a parcel will arrive the next day in France if the destination is local or within 2 days if the destination is elsewhere in France.

Chronopost can be used to send articles up to 25kg not exceeding 150cm in length and overall dimensions not exceeding 300cm. Delivery takes 24 -72 hours. Packets for outside France come in two categories: 1-2kg and parcels from 10-20kg.

Telegrams

A telegram can be sent by dialling 36 55 and reading the text to an operator. To send text in English, call 42 33 21 11 and dictate text. You can save money by using the minitel. Just call 36 56 and input text directly.

Telegrams in France cost 33frs for the first 25 words and 12frs for each additional 10 words. When using minitel, the cost is 28frs for the first 25 words and 7.50frs for each additional 10 words if you wish to send the same day or 26frs for the first 25 words and 5.50frs for each additional 10 words if input up to 40 days before it needs to be sent (e.g. for birthdays, etc.).

Telegrams destined for Europe and most major countries cost 74.75frs for the first 15 words and 24.90frs for each additional 5 words or 60frs and 19.92 per 5 words if you use the minitel.

Telecopy

A facsimile (electronic photocopy) of any document can be sent anywhere in France or worldwide. The first page costs 20frs and 10frs per subsequent page in France. An additional 21frs is payable to have the document hand delivered and another 5frs to have reception confirmed by telephone. The same service costs 30frs for the first page and 17frs per subsequent page in Europe with 70frs and 40frs being the rate to North America.

Post Office Account

The post office supplies many services usually supplied by banks like a checking account and credit card. To open an account bring along some form of identification and proof of residence (e.g. an electricity bill (EDF), a telephone bill or a rent bill showing name.

Health and Social Security

Obtain a form from Irish local Health Board which explains reciprocal agreements about health care, in EC countries. Apply for form E 111 (available from local Health Board) which entitles the holder to free medical treatment within the EEC.

In France it is necessary to produce the E 111 before treatment will be given (or by declaring it is on the way!). Unfortunately the E 111 is intended for holidaymakers only. Once employed, social security contributions are deducted from salary and employee is covered by the country's health system. Of course many casual jobs are in the black economy and employees will find that they are completely unprotected.

If sick contact a doctor or hospital agreed by the Social Security *(conventionné)*, e.g. *SOS Médecins* (doctors), tel 47 07 77 77; *SOS Dentaire* (dentists) 43 37 51 00. SOS HELP, tel 47 23 80 80, is an English-speaking telephone listening service. Provides psychological support and practical advice, 3-11pm.

Emergency medical care

Accidents

For serious injuries (broken limbs, choking, burns, etc.): dial 17 *Police Secours* any time of day or night. They respond to any medical emergency with a doctor and a fully equipped ambulance if necessary by means of their *Service d'Aide Médicale d'Urgence (SAMU)*, dial 15 or18. They provide transportation for any sick person to the nearest French hospital for immediate attention. The *Pompiers* and *Police Secours* are authorized only to take the sick person to the nearest French general hospital *(Assistance Publique)*.

If *Police Secours* do not reply, dial 18, *Pompiers* (Fire Department) any time of day or night. Ask for the physician on duty *(Médecin regulateur)* who will inform what measures to take. The *Pompiers* give artificial respiration and provide oxygen.

These numbers are usually found in the centre of the telephone dial. If not, write them and keep them by the telephone or taped to it. There is no charge for services provided by the *Pompiers* or *Police Secours*.

Important: For use in an emergency, write out proper name, address and telephone number and tape them to the telephone. Learn a few basic phrases in French to use in an emergency.

Illness

For emergencies telephone 43 37 77 77 or SOS 77 77 (47 07 77 77), *SOS Médecins* circulate in radio-equipped cars throughout Paris. The fees vary according to the extent and kind of treatment provided, but count 170frs (day), 235frs (night) and 275frs (Sunday) for the doctor's visit.

Hospital and Clinics

French general hospitals *(assistance publique)* are good, with high medical standards. In general, hospitals are preferable to private clinics because the former are normally better equipped. Some clinics may have more attractive rooms but the service is not necessarily better and the treatment is often more expensive than in hospitals. Check to see if expenses incurred at a clinic are reimbursable by the Social Security. Be prepared to make a down payment for surgery or other major services when entering the hospital. Some *assistance publique* hospitals also have private wards which are more expensive and more comfortable.

Local pharmacy will provide advice and information on nearby facilities.
e.g. *Hôpital International de l'Université de Paris*, 42 bd Jourdan, 75014 Paris, tel 45 89 47 8

Hôpital Necker des Enfants Malades, 149-151 rue de Sevres, 75015 Paris tel 42 73 80 00 (bring a sick child here as staff are specially trained).

Hertford British Hospital, 48 rue de Villiers,92300 Levallois-Perret tel 47 58 13 12 (English spoken).

For Irish doctors, see *Useful addresses.*

Pharmacies

Look for a green-cross neon sign which is switched on during opening hours. If closed, a notice on the door will indicate the nearest open pharmacy. A list of *Pharmacies de garde* tells which pharmacies are open on any given day. At night or on Sunday the local police station will give the address of the nearest open pharmacy.

Pharmacie 'Les Champs', 84 av des Champs-Elysées, 75008 Paris, tel 42 56 02 41 (Open day and night, Sundays and holidays).

Note: Tape the price tags *(vignettes)* of medicines on your social-security form, in order to be reimbursed by Social Security.

First aid is always available at any pharmacy. French pharmacists will provide care for such minor emergencies as burns, shock, sprains, etc. This is lawful and do not hesitate to request such help, if the condition is not serious enough to warrant the immediate attention of a doctor.

The local pharmacy keeps a list of nearby doctors, dentists, clinics, and nurses (who make home visits).

Dental Care

Emergency

S.O.S. Dentaire, 85 bd Port Royal,75013 Paris,tel 43 37 51 00
Open by appointment 8-12am every day including Saturday and Sunday. After noon, an appointment may be made for the following day. House calls 7pm-midnight.

Conseil de l'ordre des chirurgiens-dentistes, Paris and northern suburb (Seine-St. Denis),tel 43 61 12 00
A recording line lists dentists on call.

Höpital La Pitié-Salpetrière, Service de Stomatologie, tel 45 70 21 12
24-hour dental coverage.

For Irish dentists see *Useful addresses.*

Social Security *(Securité Sociale)*

Registration with the French Social Security is obligatory for all working persons. Advice should always be sought at employer's Business Office. It is their function to clarify and explain such issues.

Registration: Within eight days of starting work, an employer is bound by French law to declare his employee to the Social Security system. An officially translated copy of long-form birth certificate (bearing an Irish Embassy stamp) must be sent with the declaration.

For workers who are being registered for the first time, a receipt with a temporary number will be received and this must be kept until a social security card with a permanent number is received.

Reimbursements will not be received from social security until:
-a temporary number has been received.
-a total of (at least) 120 hours in the month or 200 hours a quarter have been completed at work.

Refunds: To receive a refund of medical expenses from the social security office, the following is necessary:
-In the case of illness lasting more than 48 hours, it is obligatory to have an *arrêt de travail* signed by an attending doctor. This must be sent immediately to local social security office (depending on place of residence) and also to employer. The same procedure must be followed in the case of prolonged illness.
-On returning to work, employee will receive a statement from employer to receive the necessary cash benefits.
-In order to receive the refund, send to the social security office:
*the completed certificate *(feuille de maladie)* signed by the doctor, as well as any medical prescriptions received. On the prescription form it will be necessary to attach the small price/code number stickers on the medicine boxes *(vignettes)*;
*justification of length of time employed (monthly pay slips).

Amount of Reimbursements: In general, 70% - 80% of expenses are reimbursed, unless expenses were paid to doctors or dentists who have not signed a contract with the Social Security *(convention)*, e.g. some homeopaths, some acupuncturists. It is wise to check before treatment.
NB: There is a ceiling on reimbursements.

The first three days of sickness [waiting period] are not reimbursed. The following days are reimbursed up to 50%, limited by the ceiling imposed by Social Security.

Accidents: In the event of an accident at work,or on the way to or from work, employer's business office should be contacted as soon as possible in order to give necessary details of the accident to the social security office.

Other Benefits: Social Security pays other benefits to families of persons employed in France, regardless of income or nationality:

a) family allowance   d) single income
b) maternity allowance   e) housing allowance
c) moving allowance   f) old age pension/insurance

After certain operations, up to one month convalesence in a nursing home is also provided. There is a nominal charge of about 35frs a day. Information must be provided by employer.

Voluntary Health Insurance *(Mutuel)*

All non-wage earning students who do not enjoy the benefits of Social Security *must* under French law take out social insurance for themselves and their dependants. This must be done *before* they register for university or other third-level courses. They can *not* apply for a *carte de séjour* without having acquired student insurance *(la mutuelle étudiante)*

SEM/USEM *(Société des Etudiants Mutualistes, membre de l'Union Nationale des Société Etudiantes Mutualistes Régionales)* offers three different policies ranging from 3,000-3,500frs p.a. (Payment may be made per trimester). Each policy covers medical expenses and accident liabilities. Medical expenses include doctor's fees, pharmaceutical, dental, hospital (incl. surgical) and ophthalmic costs. Accident liabilities cover those caused by the insured as well as those suffered. Medical cover extends from 75-100% of expenses. A policy may be taken out to cover pregnancy but only applies to planned pregnancy and *mutuelle* must be informed 10 months before the expected birth. Full details from:

SEM/USEM   SEM/USEM
B.P. 519 Paris Denfert Rochereau,   10 rue Remy Dumoncel,
75666 Paris, Cedex 14 *(courrier)*   75014 Paris *(accueil)*
                                tel 43 27 81 56

All workers are advised to join a *Société Mutuelle* (VHI type organisations which provide complementary insurance). The *Mutuels* help to make up the difference between reimbursement from *Securité Sociale* and actual expenses. Loans may also be obtained from some *Mutuels*. Different societies specialise in different professions and trades.

Useful Terminology
ambulance - ambulance
assistance publique - general hospital
assurance - insurance
chirurgien - surgeon
clinique - clinic
dentiste - dentist
feuille de maladie - doctor's certificate
hôpital - hospital
infirmière - nurse
malade - sick
médecin - doctor
mutuel - voluntary health insurance
pharmacie - chemist shop
poison - poison
police secours - paramedical police
pompiers - firemen
securité sociale - social security
vignettes - price tags

Further information:
Health Care Resources in Paris (American University of Paris)

Religion

Church Services in English

Catholic

Chapelle St Patrick
5 rue des Irlandais,
75005 Paris
M° Place Monge,
Cardinal Lemoine,
RER Luxembourg

Sunday Mass 11.30am
Confession Sundays 11-11.30am
Baptisms during Sunday Mass
First Communion Class
Counselling by appointment
Special celebrations: St Brigid, 1 Feb,
St Patrick, 17 Mar, Feast of the Irish
Saints, 6 Nov, Christmas Carols,
mid-Dec

Irish Chaplain:
Fr. Liam Swords tel 43 31 32 65

St. Joseph's Church
50 Av Hoche
75008 Paris
M° Charles-de-Gaulle Etoile

Fr Paul Francis Spencer CP
Fr Anthony Behan CP
Fr Brendan McKeever
tel 42 27 28 56

Masses:
Sat 11am, 6.30pm
Sun 9.45, 11am, 12.15, 6.30pm
Mon-Fri 8.30am
Confessions:
Sat 11am-12.30pm
(and by appointment)
CCD - Sundays 11am

Foyer Notre Dame
26bis rue de Lubeck
75016 Paris
M° Iéna
tel 47 27 49 15 (Convent)
45 53 62 86 (Hostel)
Sr Elizabeth, Sr Kathleen, Sr Gertrude, Secretary.

Daily Mass 9am
Weds 8.30pm
Evening Prayer
and Rosary 6pm
Office hours: Mon-Fri:
9am-12.30pm and 2-6pm

Other Christian Churches

American Cathedral in Paris
23 av George V
75008 Paris
M° George V, Alma Marceau
tel 47 20 17 92

Services:
Sun 9, 11am,
(Sun school/,
nursery)
Weekdays 12am

American Church in Paris
65 Quai d'Orsay
75007 Paris
M° Invalides,
Alma Marceau
tel 47 05 07 99

Services:
Sun 10,11am
(Sunday school
beginning 11.20)

St George's Church
(Anglican/Episcopalian)
7 rue Auguste Vacquerie
75116 Paris
M° Etoile, Kléber, George V

Services:
Sun 8.30,10.30am (S.Sch & crêche)
6.30pm (Evensong)
Weekdays: Call for times.
tel 47 20 22 51

St Michael's Church
(Anglican/Episcopalian)
5 rue d'Aguesseau
75008 Paris
M° Concorde,
Madeleine
tel 47 42 70 88

Services:
Sunday 10.30,11.45am
6.30pm
(Crèche at all services)
Thursday - lunchtime
service

The Scots Kirk
(Church of Scotland/
Presbyterian)
 17 rue Bayard
75008 Paris
M° Franklin D. Roosevelt
tel 48 78 47 94

Service:
Sun10.30am(and Sun Sch)

Useful Terminology

abbé - priest
acte de baptême - baptismal certificate
aumônier - chaplain
baptême - baptism
Catholique - Catholic
curé - parish priest
église - church
laïque - lay person
Messe - Mass
pasteur - pastor
pratiquant(e) - Church-goer
prière - prayer
Protestant(e) - Protestant
quête - collection
vicaire- curate

Statutory Rights

Contracts

If after working for three months in a fulltime job without a written contract, upon issue of third pay slip the employee automatically has an unlimited contract with that employer.
- unlimited contract *(contrat à durée indeterminée-CDi)*
- limited contracts *(contrat à durée determinée)*
- youth training or professional training contracts

Unlimited contract is the classic type which defines the position offered, any trial periods and remuneration.

A limited contract:
- not more than 3 contracts may be offered
- the period of time of a second or third may not be longer than the previous original contract

- in total, all three contracts must be no longer than 24 months
- at the end a bonus of 5% must be given on top of all salary and holiday pay earned.

The third is a contract with an element of training, often government subsidised *(stage)*. The better kind entails an already more serious job and thus the commitment and need of the employer to invest in his own staff.

Resignation and Lay off

For the CDi the employee has to give 1-2 months notice depending on the position held or the convention in the profession.

If employed in a company for more than two years, the employee is entitled to a percentage of his/her total earnings to date in the event of being layed off.

Holidays

The employee is entitled to 2.5 days per month holidays with full pay. These days are accumulated over a calendar year running from June to May of the following year, e.g. if employee joins a company in July 1990, he/she cannot avail of 2.5 days per month accumulated until June 1991. If he/she joins in April, 1990 he/she can avail of 2.5 days accumulated in June 1990, two months later. For the purposes of calculation Saturdays are counted as working days so there are five weeks holidays.Normally, there is no payment in lieu of holidays except on resignation or being layed off.

Public Holidays

New Years Day, 1 Jan	Easter Monday
Workers' Day, 1 May	Victory Day, 8 May
Ascension Thursday	Whit Monday
Bastille Day, 14 July	Assumption, 15 Aug
All Saints, 1 Nov	Armistice Day, 11 Nov
Christmas Day, 25 Dec	

Unemployment Benefits

To qualify an employee must:
- have become unemployed through no fault of his/her own (resignees receive nothing)
- register with ANPE and ASSEDIC as an unemployed person seeking work
- have evidence of periods working in France or in the EEC (E301) if applicable -
- have been working at least 6 months prior to claiming unemployment.

EC Regulation
If unemployed and receiving unemployment benefit in Ireland for at least 4 weeks, ask Department of Social Welfare to have benefit transferred to France. In France, register as unemployed within 7 days and Irish benefit will be paid each week for 13 weeks.

Basic Allowance: A variable amount equal to 47% of last average wage during the six months preceding unemployment.

Disability Benefit/Sick Pay
Social insurance paid in two or more member states of EC may be combined in order to qualify for benefit. The country in which the last contribution was paid, actually pays the benefit. Apply to the social security authorities n the country in which you become ill. If you want to live in another member state while receiving benefit, you may have your benefit transferred, provided you get authorization in advance from the country paying the benefit.

Tourism

Museums

Musée du Louvre, rue du Rivoli, tel 40 20 51 51, M° Palais-Royal/Musée du Louvre Open 9am- 6pm (closed Tuesday) late night Wednesday until 9.45pm. Admission free under-18, 30frs for adults, 15frs for 18/25 and over 60. Contains many world-famous works e.g. Mona Lisa, Venus de Milo etc and outstanding collections of Egyptian, Greek and Roman antiquities.

Musée d'Orsay, 1 rue Bellechasse, tel 40 49 48 48, M° Solférino. Open 10am-6pm (closed Monday) late night Thursday until 9.45pm. Admission free under-18, 30frs for adults. 19th and 20th century paintings with good collection of French Impressionists.

Hôtel Carnavalet, (musée de l'histoire de Paris), 23 rue de Sévigné, tel 42 72 21 13, M° Saint-Paul, open 10am-5.45pm (closed

Monday). Admission 15frs, reduced rate 8.50frs. Historical collections of prints of Paris and the French Revolution.

Musée Picasso, Hôtel Salé, 5 rue de Thorigny, tel 42 71 25 21, M° Chemin Vert/Saint Paul), Open 9.15am-5.15pm (closed Tuesday), admission 28frs, reduced rate16frs. Late night Wednesday until 10pm.

Musée Rodin, 77 rue de Varenne, tel 47 05 01 34, M° Varenne, open 10am-5pm (closed Monday), admission 20frs, half-price 10frs. Some of Rodin's most famous sculptors e.g. 'The Thinker'

Musée de Cluny, 6 place Paul-Painlevé, tel 43 25 62 00, M° Cluny, open 9.30am-5.15pm (closed Tuesday), admission 16frs, reduced rate and Sundays 8frs, Free under-18. Medieval and Renaissance collections.

Musée des Arts Décoratifs,107 rue de Rivoli, tel 42 60 32 14, M° Palais-Royal, open 12.30pm-6pm and on Sundays from midday to 6pm (closed Monday and Tuesday), Admission 23frs, reduced rate 14frs. Medieval, Renaissance, Louis XIV, Louis XV, 19th century and contemporary.

Orangerie des Tuileries, Place de la Concorde, tel 42 97 48 16, M° Concorde, open 9.45am-5.15pm (closed Tuesday), admission 23frs, reduced rate Sundays, 18-25, over-60, 12frs. Interesting collection of French Impressionists.

Centre National d'Art et de Culture Georges Pompidou, rue Rambuteau, tel 42 77 12 33, M° Rambuteau, open 12 midday to 10pm and Sat. Sun. and holidays, 10am-10pm, admission free. Street theatre, good library and changing exhibitions.

Grand Palais, av du Général Eisenhower, tel 42 89 23 13, M° Champs-Elyisées-Clemenceau, open 10am-6pm, late night Wednesday to 10pm, (closed Tuesday), admission 37frs, reduced rate and Sat. 24frs. Holds important temporary exhibitions.

Petit Palais, av Winston-Churchill, tel 42 65 12 73, M° Champs-Elysées-Clemenceau, open 10am-5.40pm,(closed Monday), admission 12frs, reduced rate 6frs. Museum of Fine Arts of the city of Paris.

Cité des Sciences et de l'Industrie - La Villette, 30 av Corentin-Cariou, tel 40 05 70 00, M° Porte de La Villette, open 10am-6pm,(closed Mon), admission 35frs, reduced rate 25frs. The city of the 21st century.

Musée Grévin, 10 bd Montmartre, tel 47 70 85 05, M° rue Montmartre, open 1-7pm, admission 46frs, children 32frs. Waxwork museum.

Monuments

Arc de Triomphe, place de l'Etoile, open 10am-5.30pm, admission 30frs,reduced rate 16frs.

Notre Dame de Paris, place du Parvis Notre Dame, M° Cité, RER Saint Michel-Notre Dame, Cathedral open 8am-7pm, Tower and Crypt, open 10am-5pm, admission, combined 40frs.

Sacre-Coeur, 35 rue du Chevalier-de-la-Barre, M° Anvers, Basilica open, 7am-12pm, Dome and Crypt, open 9am-7pm, admission 15frs.

Tour Eiffel, Champs-de-Mars, M° Bir Hakeim, RER Champs-de-Mars, 9.30am-11pm, admission, 4th floor/49frs, 3rd floor/32frs, 2nd floor/17frs, reduced rates for children under 12.

Panthéon, place du Panthéon, RER Luxembourg, open 10am-12am, 2pm-7pm, admission 24frs, reduced rate 13frs.

Sainte-Chapelle, 4 bd du Palais, M° Cité, open 10am-5pm, admission 24frs.

Conciergerie, 1 quai de l'Horloge, M° Cité, open 9.30-6.30, admission 24frs.

Tour Montparnasse, (panoramic view), open 10am-10pm, admission 35frs.

Grande Arche de la Défense, parvis de la Défense, RER La Défense, open Mon-Fri 9am-5pm, Sat,Sun, holidays 10am-5pm, admission 30frs.

Bus Tours

Cityrama, 4 place des Pyramides, 42 60 30 14, M°Palais Royal

Excursions Parisiennes, 51 rue Maubeuge, M° Cadet

France Tourisme/Paris Vision, 214 rue de Rivoli, M° Tuileries

RATP Bus N°63, Gare de Lyon-La Muette, scenic route along the Seine and Boulevard Saint-Germain-des-Près

Bus N°27, Porte de Vitry-Gare Saint-Lazare crossing the city between Luxembourg and Opéra

Montmartrebus from Pigalle to M° Jules Joffrin through the charming narrow streets of Montmartre around Sacre Coeur.

Boat Trips

Bateaux-Mouches, pont de l'Alma, M° Alma-Marceau, 10am-11pm, every half-hour, 75mins trip, 30frs.

Bateaux Parisiens Notre Dame, quai de Montebello, RER Saint-Michel, every hour from 10am-10pm, 60mins trip.

Bateaux vedettes du Pont Neuf, square du Vert-Galant, M° Pont-Neuf,every 30mins from 10am-12am and 1.30pm-6.30pm, 60mins trip, 35frs

Bateaux Parisiens Tour Eiffel, Port de la Bourdonnais, M° Trocadéro, every hour from 10am-9pm, 60mins trip, 35frs

Walks

Ile St-Louis, Ile de la Cité, Notre-Dame, medieval Paris, the geographic and historic heart of Paris. Here in the 1st century the Gallo-Romans built the city they called Lutetia.

Opéra, Paris of the *belle époque*. Haussmann created the *grands boulevards* which surround the Opéra.

Montmartre is a village perched high over Paris giving a panoramic view from the steps of Sacré-Coeur. Place du Tertre is full of artists and surrounded by picturesque narrow streets.

Latin Quarter is the student quarter and so-called because students spoke Latin here. The hill of Mont Sainte-Geneviève was dotted with the colleges of the university including Collège des Lombards and Collège des Irlandais and of course the oldest and most famous college, the Sorbonne. Visit also rue Mouffetard with its charming street market.

The Marais with its charming Place des Vosges, recently restored, represents XVII century Paris and the period of *The Three Muskateers*.

Parks and Gardens

Jardin des Plantes, M° Gare d'Austerlitz/Jussieu, botannical gardens with little zoo.

Jardin du Luxembourg, RER Luxembourg, with its 17th century Medicis fountain. Palais du Luxembourg now houses the French senate.

Tuileries Gardens, a vast formal garden, designed by Le Nôtre, extending from the Louvre to Place de la Concorde.

Bois de Boulogne, vast park of over 2000 acres, with 7 lakes, Longchamp racetrack, and Bagatelle in its NW corner.

Parc de Monceau, M° Monceau, tree-shaded park with pagodas and oriental art museum.

Cemeteries

Père-Lachaise, M° Père-Lachaise. Chopin, Molière, Sarah Bernhardt, Balzac, Isadora Duncan, Oscar Wilde, Edith Piaf, Jim Morrison etc buried here

Montparnasse, M° Raspail, with the tombs of Sartre, Maupassant, Baudelaire, Serge Gainsbourg, Samuel Beckett etc

Montmartre, M° Place de Clichy, has the graves of Dégas, Offenbach, Nijinski, Berlioz, Fragonard and Wexford '98 rebel, Myles Byrne.

Entertainment

Reviews

A complete guide to all entertainment in Paris can be found in two weekly reviews which appear every Wednesday and can be bought at any street kiosk, *Pariscope*, 3frs and *l'Officiel des Spectacles*, 2frs.

Theatres

Comedie Française, 2 rue de Richelieu, tel 40 15 00 15, M° Palais-Royal, admission, 45-195frs

Opéra Bastille, place de la Bastille, tel 40 01 16 16, M° Bastille, admission, opera/40-520frs, concerts/50-280frs

Opéra Garnier, place de l'Opéra, tel 47 42 53 71, M° Opéra, admission 30-350frs

Orchestral concerts take place in many of the Parisian churches, admission 90frs, though some are free, e.g. Saint-Médard, Saint-Merri and the organ recital in Notre-Dame, every Sunday at 5.15pm

Cinemas

There are 300 films on show each week in Paris and its suburbs. These are classified alphabetically in the weekly reviews, with a short resumé of each film, as well as by cinema and location. Address is given and nearest Métro with starting times of *séance* (show) and film. A large selection of foreign-language films are available with subtitles in French. Watch out for the designation v.o. *(version originale)* which indicates that an English-language film will be in English and foreign-language in its original language with French subtitles. Admission, 40frs (approx) with reduction, 30frs (approx) on Mondays.

Night-Clubs

Le Lido, 116 bis av Champs-Elysées, tel 40 76 56 10, dinner/show, 8pm, 605frs, champagne/show, 10pm, 420frs

Moulin Rouge, place Blanche, tel 46 06 00 19, dinner/show, 8pm, 605frs, champagne/show, 10pm, 420frs

Crazy Horse, 12 av George-V, tel 47 23 32 32, 2 drinks show, 9pm and 11.35pm, prices from 510-380frs

Paradis Latin, 28 rue du Cardinal-Lemoine, tel 43 25 28 28, dinner/show, 8pm, 605frs, champagne/show, 10pm, 420frs

Day Trips

Versailles, RER line C from Paris to Versailles Rive Gauche, 12frs. Trip 40 mins and 15min walk to 17th century chateau of Louis XIV. Open 9.45am-5pm.

Saint-Germain-en-Laye, RER line A, chateau beside station, with magnificent Le Nôtre garden and panoramic view of Paris and the Seine. Louis XIV gave the chateau to James 11 after the Battle of the Boyne

Giverny, Claude Monet's home, gardens, and oft-painted lily-ponds, half-way between Paris and Rouen. Train from Gare Saint-Lazare to Vernon, and bus, taxi or bicycle, for 3 miles to Giverny. Open 1 April-31 Oct, 10-12am, 2-6pm (closed Mondays)

Chartres, 12th century cathedral. Train from Gare Montparnasse to Chartres which takes about 1hr

Chantilly, late 19th century chateau with gardens landscaped by Le Nôtre. Also a famous race-course with *Musée Vivant du Cheval*. Train from Gare du Nord takes about 30mins

Malmaison, the chateau given by Napoleon to Josephine. RER line A to La Défense, 158A bus to Bois Preu (closed Tuesdays)

Fontainebleau, renaissance palace and last home of Napoleon. Train from Gare de Lyon takes approximately 40mins (closed Tuesdays)

Barbizon, village where Rousseau, Millet, Corot and others came to paint the surrounding forests and farms. Train from Gare de Lyon to Fontainebleau and bus, 2.20pm to Barbizon and returning at 5.26pm.

Leaving Paris

Leaving Paris is not quite as complicated as moving in, although certain arrangements have to be started two or three months before the date of departure.

Giving Notice

Flat
First, three months notice must be given on rented accommodation in order to recover the deposit *(caution)*. Occasionally, at the discretion of the landlord, one month will suffice for furnished accommodation. Problems can arise with getting a deposit refunded. The landlord must reimburse the deposit within two months, less deductions for damage caused. All deductions must be justified and a copy of the repair bill provided. Repainting and other general maintenance work is not deductable.

Job

In general, two months notice is enough for jobs but sometimes three is required. The employee is entitled to two hours off per day for the last month in order to find another job. If this time is not used it is not paid in lieu. No holidays may be taken during the period. Holidays not taken are paid.

Telephone

The telephone company (France *Telecom*) and electricity and gas (EdF-GdF) should be informed about two weeks before departure in order to establish a final bill and arrange for disconnection.

Banks

Banks have no set notice period but accounts are rarely closed before departure as there are often outstanding bills and/or interest payments. A letter is sufficient to close an account. Although it can be useful to retain an account in France, those unused for two years will be moved to a special section for inactive accounts and charges will be made when the account is re-activated. Avoid this if possible.

Social Security

The Social Security office does not need to be informed of departure, but it is a good idea to keep the card so as to have the number handy if returning to France. To transfer dole benefit to another EC country, get form (E303) from local social security centre. This takes about four weeks to process.

Personal Belongings

The Irish Embassy will provide a form for importing personal belongings to Ireland (*Importation of Personal Property without Payment of Import Charges under the Transfer of Residence Provisions*). The form should be presented at Customs at the time of entry into Ireland. Luxury items such as televisions, videos and cars are not tax exempt unless more than six months old. *Note:* The television/ video system in mainland Europe is SECAM while that in Ireland and England is PAL. These two systems are not compatible, so it is best to resell SECAM equipment in France. Dual or Multi-standard equipment is widely available.

Removal

Logistic Air Sea France (LASF), tel 48 62 80 42/48 62 82 25, will pick up and deliver goods to the airport, price 159frs. Customs etc costs 300frs. Air-freight: 45-100kgs, 12.85frs per kg. 100kgs +, 8.75frs per kg.

Animals

Animals are not allowed into Ireland except after six months quarantine and a course of rabies vaccinations. Quarantine *is not free*, in fact it is quite expensive (about £500).

Bills

Outstanding bills such as income tax, property tax and television licence should of course be settled before leaving. An appointment can be made with the local branch of the Inland Revenue (Trésor Public) for taxes (address supplied on official correspondence) and the Centre de la Redevance Audiovisuel for TV (address and telephone on annual bill). A hefty fine is imposed on tax dodgers.

The residence permit does not have to be returned, but can be handed in to the prefecture which issued it.

Death in France

Where a body is to be repatriated, friends or relatives should contact the local undertakers (*pompes funebres générales*) and nominate a funeral undertaker in Ireland. Between them, undertakers should be able to take care of all practical and administrative matters concerning the repatriation. Before a body can be removed from France two certificates must be obtained, a death certificate (*acte de décès*) and a burial certificate (*certificat d'inhumation*). The former is obtained from the local *mairie* and the latter from the nearest *sous-préfecture*. In certain circumstances, a police investigation is initiated by an *inspecteur de police*, in which case, no burial certificate will be issued until after a coroner (*médecin-légiste*) presents his report to the the proscutor(*Procureur de la République*). This may involve a delay of a few days.

Irish Pubs

Au Caveau Montpensier, rue Montpensier, 75001 Paris,
tel 47 03 33 78 M° Palais Royal

Au Gobelet d'Argent, 11 rue du Cygne, 75001 Paris,
tel 42 33 29 82 M° Etienne Marcel

Bistrot Irlandais (Ryan's Pub), 15 rue de la Santé, 75013 Paris,
tel 47 07 07 45 RER Port Royal

Carr's Restaurant, 1 rue Mont Thabor, 75001 Paris, tel 42 60 60 26
M° Tuileries, Concorde

Connolly's Corner, 12 rue de Mirbel, 75005 Paris, tel 43 31 94 22
M° Censier Daubenton

Cruiskeen Lawn, 18 rue des Halles, 75001 Paris, tel 45 08 99 15,
M° Châtelet

Finnegan's Wake, 9 rue des Boulangers, 75005 Paris,
tel 46 34 23 65 M° Jussieu, Cardinal Lemoine

Flann O'Brien, 6 rue Bailleul, 75001 Paris, tel 42 60 13 58, M° Louvre

James Joyce, 5 rue du Jour, 75001 Paris, tel 45 08 17 04, M° Halles

Kitty O'Shea's, 10 rue des Capucines, 75001 Paris, tel 40 15 08 08
M° Opéra

Molly Malones, 21 rue Godot de Maur, 75019 Paris, tel 47 42 07 77
M° Madeleine

Oscar Wilde, 38 rue Bourdonnais, 75001 Paris, tel 42 21 03 63,
M° Châtelet

Stolly's, 16 rue Cloche-Perce, 75004 Paris, tel 42 76 06 76,
M° Saint-Paul

Sweeney, 18 rue Laplace, 75005 Paris, tel 46 33 28 12
M° Maubert-Mutualité

The Quiet Man, 5 rue des Haudriettes, 75003 Paris, tel 48 04 02 77
M° Rambuteau, Hôtel de Ville

Tigh Johnny, 55 rue Montmartre, 75002 Paris, tel 42 33 91 33
M° Sentier

Pub St. Michel ~ Quai st michel
~ Place st. Michel

Useful Addresses

Aer Lingus, 47 av de l'Opéra, 75002 Paris, tel 47 42 12 50 M° Opéra

Aéroport Roissy Charles de Gaulle, tel 48 62 12 12

Aéroport Orly Sud/Ouest, tel 48 84 52 52

Accueil des Jeunes en France, (AJF), Gare du Nord, Halle des Arrivées, 75010 Paris, tel 42 85 86 19 M° Gare du Nord

Alcoholics Anonymous, 3 rue Frédéric Sauton, 75005 Paris. tel 43 25 75 00/43 25 76 03 (24hrs) M° Maubert-Mutualité (10am-10pm). English speaking contact, tel 46 34 59 65

Alliance Française, 101 bd Raspail, 75006 Paris, tel 45 44 38 28 M° Rennes

American Church, 65 Quai d'Orsay, 75007 Paris, tel 47 05 07 99
M° Invalides

Archives Nationales, 56 rue des Francs-Bourgeois, 75003 Paris,
M° St Paul

Ashling Microsystems SARL, 2 rue de Tocqueville, Parc d'Activités
Antony 2, 92183 Antony, tel 46 66 27 50

Association Irlandaise, c/o Michel Sikiotakis, tel 43 49 37 48

Association pour le logement des étudiants et des jeunes travailleurs, 12-14 rue de l'Eglise, 75015 Paris, tel M° Felix Faure

AUMP, Association of Parisian Doctors for Emergencies, tel 48 28 40 04

Bibliothèque Nationale, 58 rue Richelieu, 75008 Paris M° Palais
Royal

Bórd Fáilte, Maison d'Irlande, 33 rue du Miromesnil, 75008 Paris
tel 47 42 32 55 M° Miromesnil

British Institute, 9 rue de Constantine, 75007 Paris, tel 45 55 95 95
M° Invalides

British Hospital, 3 rue Barbes, 92300 Levallois-Perret, tel 47 57 24 10

CARA Voyages, 47 av de l'Opéra, 75002 Paris, tel 47 42 10 64
M° Opéra

CBF Irlande, 138 rue du Fbg St Honoré, 75008 Paris, tel 42 25 65 70
M° St Philippe du Roule

Centre d'Affairs Irlandais, (Irish Business Center), 2 rue Alexis de
Tocqueville, Parc d'Activités, Antony 2, 92183 Antony, tel 46 66 27 50

CIE Tours International, 47 rue des Mathurins, 75008 Paris,
tel 47 42 52 29 M° Havre-Caumartin

CIDJ, 101 quai Branly, 75015 Paris, tel 45 66 4020 M° Bir-Hakeim

Collège des Irlandais, 5 rue des Irlandais, 75005 Paris,
tel 45 35 59 79/ 47 07 31 33, Residents, 43 36 45 78,
M° Place Monge, Cardinal Lemoine, RER Luxembourg

00 – 33 – 1 Res
code 1569.

Comité France-Irlande, 1 rue Auguste Vacquerie, 75016 Paris,
tel 47 20 93 90

Dwyer, Dr James, GP, 178 rue Legendre, 75017 Paris, tel 42 26 79 67,
M° Guy-Môquet

Etudes Irlandaises, rue de l'Ecole de Médecine, 75005 Paris
M° Odéon

Foyer Notre Dame, 26bis rue de Lubeck, 75016 Paris, tel 47 27 49 15
M° Iéna

Irish Chaplain /Fr. Liam Swords, 5 rue des Irlandais,75005 Paris,
tel 43 31 32 65 M° Place Monge, Cardinal Lemoine, RER Luxembourg

Irish Continental Ferries, 8 rue Auber, 75009 Paris, tel 42 66 90 90
M° Opéra

Irish Embassy, 12 av Foch (entrance, 4 rue Rude), 75016 Paris,
tel 45 00 20 87 M° Charles-de-Gaulle Etoile

Kepak-Meat production and distribution, 2 rue Alexis de Tocqueville, Parc d'Activités Antony 2, 92183 Antony, tel 46 66 26 52

Le Trefle Bleu (Irish association of Paris policemen), c/o Gérard Poucetoux, 3 rue St Nicolas, 75012 Paris

Maison d'Irlande, 33 rue Miromesnil, 75008 Paris, tel 47 42 32 55
M° Miromesnil

Pharmacie 'Les Champs', (open 24hrs), 84 av Champs Elysées, tel 42 56 02 41 M° Franklin D Roosevelt

POLICE SECOURS, tel 17

POMPIERS, tel 18

Préfecture de Police (section CCE), 93 av Parmentier, 75011 Paris, M° Parmentier

SEM/USEM, 10 rue Remy Dumoncel, 75014 Paris, tel 43 27 81 86 M° Alésia

Sorbonne, *Cours de Civilisation Française*, Galerie Richelieu, 47 rue des Ecoles, 75005 Paris, tel 40 46 22 11 ext 2664/75 RER St Michel

St Joseph's Church, 50 av Hoche, 75008 Paris, tel 42 27 28 56 M° Charles-de-Gaulle Etoile

SAMU, tel 15

Skehan, Dr Mark (Irish Obstetrician and Gynaecologist), L'Hopital Britannique, 3 rue Barbes, Levallois-Peerret, tel 47 58 13 12, M° Anatole France

Slattery, Dr Francis, (Irish GP), 42 rue de Bellechasse, 75007 Paris, tel 45 55 16 52 M° Solferino

SOS Dentaire, tel 43 37 51 00

SOS Femmes battues (battered wives), tel 47 36 96 48

SOS Médecins, tel 43 37 77 77/47 07 77 77

Steite, Dr P (Irish Dentist), 2 av de Frances Montigny les Cormeilles, tel 34 50 16 16

UNESCO, 9 Place Fontenoy, 75007 Paris, tel 45 68 00 00 M° Ségur

USIT, 6 rue Vaugirard, 75005 Paris,tel 43 29 85 00 RER Luxembourg